THE
LAST
SECRET
AGENT

THE
LAST
SECRET
AGENT

MY LIFE AS A SPY BEHIND
NAZI LINES

PIPPA LATOUR

WITH JUDE DOBSON

ST. MARTIN'S PRESS
NEW YORK

First published in the United States by St. Martin's Press,
an imprint of St. Martin's Publishing Group

THE LAST SECRET AGENT. Copyright © 2024 by Pippa Latour. All rights reserved.
Printed in the United States of America. For information, address St. Martin's
Publishing Group, 120 Broadway, New York, NY 10271.

www.stmartins.com

Map by Megan van Staden

The Library of Congress Cataloging-in-Publication Data is available upon request.

ISBN 978-1-250-38434-8 (hardcover)
ISBN 978-1-250-38435-5 (ebook)

Our books may be purchased in bulk for promotional, educational,
or business use. Please contact your local bookseller or the
Macmillan Corporate and Premium Sales Department at 1-800-221-7945,
extension 5442, or by email at MacmillanSpecialMarkets@macmillan.com.

Photographs in the picture section are from the author's private collection,
unless otherwise credited. Every effort has been made to trace the owners of
copyright imagery. If you have any information concerning copyright material
in this book, please contact the publisher.

Originally published in Australia and New Zealand by Allen & Unwin

First U.S. Edition: 2025

10 9 8 7 6 5 4 3 2 1

THIS BOOK IS PIPPA'S MEMOIR AND IS BASED PRIMAR-
ily on her recollections of this period in her life, interwoven with
historical record and information from other sources where possible. Some gaps in her memory were inevitable and not all details
could be verified. Dialogue has been reconstructed in places in the
interest of the story.

FRANCE 1940-1944

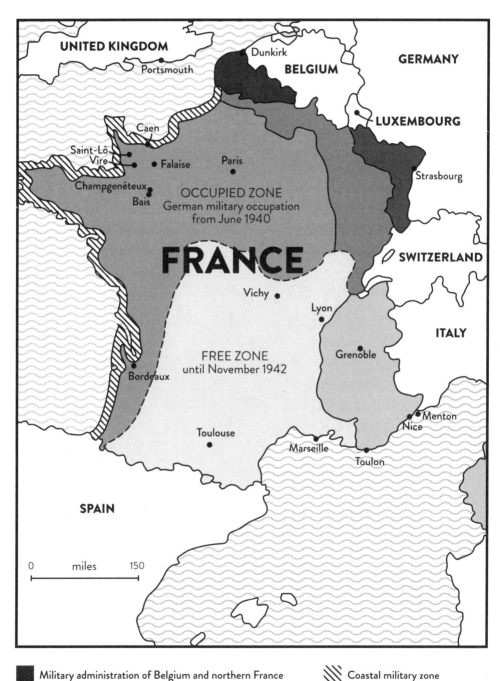

UNITED KINGDOM

Portsmouth

Dunkirk

BELGIUM

GERMANY

LUXEMBOURG

Caen

Saint-Lô
Vire

Falaise

Paris

Strasbourg

Champgenéteux
Bais

OCCUPIED ZONE
German military occupation
from June 1940

FRANCE

SWITZERLAND

Vichy

Lyon

ITALY

Grenoble

FREE ZONE
until November 1942

Bordeaux

Menton
Nice

Toulouse

Marseille

Toulon

SPAIN

0   miles   150

	Military administration of Belgium and northern France		Coastal military zone
	Territories annexed to Germany	--	Demarcation line
	Zone of German settlement		
	Italian occupation after November 1942		

CONTENTS

CONTENTS

FOREWORD

PIPPA WAS MUCH LOVED BY THE NEW ZEALAND SPE-
cial Air Service. Even though her body finally aged, her spirit never
did. I remember Pippa happily declaring, at her one-hundredth
birthday, that she had passed her medical and still had her own
driver's license. For us as special operators, it was Pippa's fiercely
independent spirit that we felt a kindred connection to, as well
as the glint in her eye. Secretly, we all hoped we might shine at
least half as brightly in our later years as she did in hers. But even
we—as fond as we were of Pippa, and as secure as our environment
is—only ever heard snippets of her story. Perhaps her great friend,
Major David Hopkins, knew more. But David, ever fiercely loyal,
would only allude to the tales of Pippa's derring-do—the details
were never divulged.

So, this book is a rare and privileged glimpse into the life of the
last surviving SOE agent to have seen action behind enemy lines in
France. In many ways it is Pippa's last public service, her last contri-
bution to freedom. It is a remarkable testament to one of the most
remarkable women I have ever met. As Selwyn Jepson, the recruiting officer for SOE F (French) Section, once said: "Women have
a greater capacity for cool and lonely courage than men." Pippa's

story, wonderfully told in the pages that follow, leaves the truth of that statement in no doubt.

In finally telling her story, Pippa does honor to the brave women in SOE and their French civilian allies who served and suffered—and in many cases, died—for our freedom. I hope that this story inspires other young people, especially young women, to take courage, to stand for what they value, and, when faced by fearful odds, to set them ablaze.

Chris Parsons MNZM DSD
Commanding Officer NZSAS (2009–2011)

PREFACE

MY NAME IS PHYLLIS ADA LATOUR, KNOWN TO MANY in my later years as Pippa, and I am 102 years old. I am also known by other names—code names and alias names—because I was a World War II secret operative agent. This is my memoir, which finally tells the story of my life working behind enemy lines in France eighty years ago. It is a part of my life that, until now, I have intentionally never revealed to anybody. Not my husband (when I had one), nor my children—even when they became adults.

It would likely have stayed that way, which would have suited me perfectly, if it were not for my eldest son finding something about me on the internet, some twenty years ago. Without the advent of the internet—something I could not have foreseen when I made the decision never to talk about these things in 1945—my wish for secrecy would likely have remained intact. Because, as I see it, it wasn't anybody's business what I did in the war. It was my business. Mine alone.

My son was prompted to discuss the discovery with his younger brother, concerned that their mother might be in some sort of trouble and that was why I had never mentioned it to them. He flew to New Zealand (where I live, as does his younger brother) to meet up with him. Together they decided to talk to me, and the two obvious questions were posed. Was this World War II operative, Phyllis Latour, their mother of the same name? And presuming that it was (as they had), why had I never mentioned this to them? I could not lie to my sons once they asked me directly. Up until then, I had simply chosen not to tell them everything about my war. Instead I had told them what I thought they needed to know. I was a balloon operator for the Women's Auxiliary Air Force (WAAF) in the Royal Air Force (RAF), and that was not incorrect: I did that job for three years. I am pretty sure I told them about my time in the Royal Navy records department before that. I just didn't tell them what came in the later stages of the war with the Special Operations Executive (SOE). And my former husband? I chose never to tell him because I saw how loose he was with quite sensitive information told to him by others. I thought if he was like that with their information, *my* information was never going to be kept secret by him.

★

BEFORE I START TELLING you about my life, you'll need some background on what SOE is. In June 1940, the Special Operations Executive was established by England's wartime prime minister, Winston Churchill, to wage a secret war using an underground army of sorts in enemy-occupied Europe and Asia. Its purpose was to conduct espionage, sabotage, and reconnaissance in occupied Europe (and, later, also in occupied Southeast Asia), as well as aiding local resistance movements. Deliberately clandestine, the existence of SOE was not widely known even though some 13,000 people were involved. About 3,200 of these people were women. I was one of the women, and my job was to be a radio operator in northern France, which I did in 1944.

Churchill instructed those, like me, tasked with the work across the English Channel to go forth and "set Europe ablaze." Sabotage and subversion behind enemy lines, and passing intelligence to Mother England, required courage, resilience, and resourcefulness from those of us who agreed to these dangerous jobs. By working with local Resistance forces, we boosted their morale through our presence on the ground. They were, rightly, wondering when and how this dreadful war would ever end.

In France, with new identities and forged papers, we SOE agents covered hundreds of miles on foot, by bike, or on trains, all the time under the constant threat of arrest by the Gestapo should our identity be blown or the work we were undertaking be discovered. It was an exhausting task, with the ongoing threat of possibly being betrayed by double agents and traitors. It was hard to trust anyone.

It was also not glamorous; don't think of me or my fellow agents as 007 types. Our job was to disappear—to fit in and not be noticed. Taking the job certainly didn't win you any friends in high places either; quite the opposite, in fact. There was plenty of tension between SOE and England's Secret Intelligence Service (SIS, now known as MI6), which the Foreign Office had to deal with. The SIS viewed SOE with some suspicion. I did not know it at the time, but Sir Stewart Menzies, head of the SIS, argued on many an occasion that SOE agents were "amateur, dangerous, and bogus," saying that we would disrupt their own intelligence-gathering operations by blowing up bridges and factories. The SIS preferred to work quietly through influential channels and individuals, whereas SOE's way of operating was more grassroots. We also often backed anti-establishment organizations, such as the communists; I could only ever really trust communists in France. I also learned after the war that Bomber Command and SOE did not always see eye to eye.

Although all these vested interests brought massive internal political pressure to bear on the fledgling organization, SOE had Churchill as its ally; "Churchill's Secret Army" not only survived, but thrived, throughout World War II. There was also resistance to our existence across in France. General de Gaulle was never keen to recognize our significance, and we definitely felt that on the ground there. Looking back, it was a strange and solitary existence I found myself in throughout 1944. I could only ever rely on myself—from the top echelons of the British establishment to the people on the ground with me in France, and everyone in between, I trusted very few people. That became ingrained in me in my early twenties as a survival instinct.

★

FAST-FORWARD SIXTY YEARS TO me in my eighties in New Zealand, where I have lived quietly for many years, keeping my head down about all that stuff. The discovery of this period of my life was a revelation to my sons, and I have to say it caused some discord. If I am honest, I think there was some resentment that their mother had actively chosen not to take them into her confidence. When confronted about that decision, I was at pains to explain that as much as I personally didn't want to talk about it, there was also something bigger behind this. I signed an oath not to disclose anything about my war service with SOE. That pledge was something I knew I must honor, and that meant not telling a living soul—not even my family. I was subject to the rules of the Official Secrets Act, and that was not something I wanted to test. The stories were known only to me and the handful of trusted people I shared that hellish existence with. I had never wanted to revisit them. I had buried them. The flashbacks that had caused me to wake up in a sweat had by then become few and far between.

After the war, I simply disappeared. Given that I'd excelled at not being noticed as a spy in wartime, it was not so difficult to fade into an anonymous postwar existence. Besides which, the whole thing had been utterly exhausting, both mentally and physically, and I was completely fed up with double agents and collaborators and trying to figure out who I could trust. I had been fighting my own war within a war—there I was in France, and I couldn't even trust the French unless they were communists. If I say that to people now, they don't really get it, but it was the truth.

After the war ended, I was ready to move on with my life and vowed I would never step foot back in France after I left there in October 1944. And I never have. I have been asked more than once if I would go back, and the answer has always been a resolute no.

While I was silent about my experience, it seems that others were not. I heard about people wanting medals for this and that, things they did in the war; people saying things that were not right; people writing things that were not right. I would simply think "Poppycock—there's more poppycock coming out!" If people are going to write things, they must tell the truth—and the truth is not pretty; it's not good.

This book tells the truth about my war. I'm the last living female special operative from F Section, and I need to record what happened before I die. I would like to leave my story behind so that, perhaps, young women in particular might know what it was like for me back then.

★

I AM PROUD OF being a woman in what was very much a man's world. Of the 430 SOE agents in France, only 39 of us were women and 14 of our group never returned. We were a mixed lot, probably because we were chosen for our language skills and therefore were not your standard English girls. We were women of various descent, among them British, French, Polish, Finnish, American, and South African, like me. We had different belief systems, too—Jewish, Muslim, Catholic, etc. Some of us were young and unmarried; others had husbands and children. Some were shop assistants; others were journalists. I had had no opportunity to even have a job because I was only eighteen when war broke out, so my vocation became "fighting a war."

What we women all had in common, though, was the knowledge that it was a dangerous job and that there was great hope from our commanders that we could do something our male counterparts could not: *survive*. We all knew that the remaining life expectancy of a male radio operator who entered occupied France was just six weeks, and on more than one occasion had it explained to us that the chances of us coming back were 50/50. It is a wonder that any of us actually agreed to the job—I am not sure people would do so today, but you have to understand that wartime is very different. We were all doing our bit, fighting for what we believed in, pushing back against a cruel and expansionist enemy.

Unlike other special forces, SOE operatives wore civilian clothes.

That fact alone meant we could expect to be shot as spies if we were captured, and we were at risk of torture by German Gestapo operatives trying to extract information. This all came from the notorious Commando Order that Hitler passed in October 1942. It decreed that any commando or saboteur taken prisoner, whether uniformed or not, would be treated as a spy—even if they had attempted to surrender. They were to be handed over immediately to the Gestapo or the SD (the abbreviation for Sicherheitsdienst, another Nazi intelligence organization) for immediate execution.

I could never escape that sobering thought. And as women there were even fewer protections for us if we were caught and survived the initial threat of execution. Many of the male SOE agents were treated much better by the German authorities than we were, because, allegedly, women were not covered by the Geneva Convention at the time. Our SOE women who died, died horrible deaths after enduring indescribable torture.

The hope, though, was that women could blend into the fabric of society better and draw less suspicion. We would also be able to move around more freely, because with so many French men of working age being sent to Germany as forced labor, any "new" men in a community were met with obvious distrust. The instruction to use women came from Churchill himself, with Selwyn Jepson, the recruiting officer for the French section of SOE, agreeing with him. After the war Jepson was quoted as saying: "In my view, women were very much better than men for the work. Women . . . have a greater capacity for cool and lonely courage than men." Many men were not of the same view as Jepson and simply did not believe that women should serve behind enemy lines. This was, as they saw it, not a place for the fairer sex, and they probably thought we weren't capable of it anyway. I, for one, felt that judgment at various points in training or on the ground and wanted to prove them wrong.

However, with intelligence-gathering from the front being so crucial to the war effort, women suddenly became useful on the front line, not just in the back room. Getting us into the thick of it was not so straightforward, though: the statutes of the British Army, Navy, and Royal Air Force barred women from armed combat, so it required a workaround by the politicians of the day. That "fix" had us joining the volunteer First Aid Nursing Yeomanry (FANY). The FANYs were an amazing group of women, and they deserve their place in history. The corps' strength in World War II was six thousand—of which two thousand were also in SOE. I could contact the SOE FANYs at any time of the day or night from occupied France, secure in the knowledge that they would be there to hear my message and respond. Wonderful women. I can't tell you how important they were to me. They were my invisible, reliable lifeline to London and a former existence that I often wondered whether I would ever be able to experience again.

★

I WAS THE FIRST (and only) woman to be dropped solo by the Americans, and just the second woman they had ever dropped. (Nancy Wake was the first, a couple of days before me.) Once there I spent my days moving from place to place, only using fellow SOE agent Claude de Baissac's Scientist network if I needed to—unlike other radio operators at that stage of the war who were mostly stationary and connected to a group. I was also one of the very last female operatives to get out of France after its liberation.

Although I still have the feeling that my wartime work is not really anybody else's business, I can see that I should tell my story before it dies with me. In 2024, when the first edition of this book comes out, it will have been eighty years since D-Day happened, and maybe there won't be too many of us left who can remember that day. I can.

I have been reassured that the Official Secrets Act is not a problem for me anymore. So, I would like to set the record straight (if it is wonky anywhere) and tell my own story; which, as I am recalling it, does not seem as long ago as it so obviously is. I appreciate that if you don't speak up, others can fill the void and say things that are not challenged, or may say things innocently while presuming them to be correct, when in fact they are not. I still do not have the internet and I don't want it. But what I do want is to have my story recorded for those people who are interested in World War II and some of the things that went on. Just to set expectations, though: if people are aware of my history, one thing they often ask is "How many Germans did you kill?" I always look them straight in the eye and say, "None."

Well, the truth is: "Not directly." I killed a lot *indirectly* with the information I messaged back to England, which then triggered air attacks. I am not sure if those people are disappointed when I answer, "None." It seems a funny thing to ask someone you don't really know. Death is traumatic—I don't have to have personally killed anyone myself to be traumatized by it. I have witnessed more than my fair share of death and destruction at very close quarters;

sometimes because of me, sometimes despite me, and sometimes just because it is Wednesday and the Gestapo have come through a village, rounded up some people randomly, and shot them dead. Remember: I was not a James Bond–style spy. I was a secret agent whose job it was to blend into the background and cause quiet chaos.

My story starts in South Africa and has traversed many countries and many names before ending up in New Zealand, 102 years later. Here, I now find myself talking about the life of one Pippa Latour, who started life as Phyllis in 1921 and embarked on an unusual childhood in Africa that set me up for an equally unusual wartime job. I think I like being a little unusual, even now. It suits me.

Pippa Latour, September 2023

THE
LAST
SECRET
AGENT

ONE

MY EARLY YEARS

I WAS BORN ON A JETTY AT THE PORT OF DURBAN, South Africa. On the morning of April 8, 1921, while still at sea off the South African coast, my mother had felt the familiar pain of the contractions of early labor. It was too early for her to be feeling them, so I am quite sure her heart fell when the odd twinge turned into something more regular, because she was only seven months pregnant. This was a risky situation for both mother and baby.

It must surely have crossed my mother's mind that I might enter the world earlier than was ideal, given that I was her third child and both of her previous babies had arrived before their due dates. Still, these things are not always predictable and perhaps she thought "third time lucky"—this baby might make it to nine months before wanting to be born. Alas, that was not to be the case. Although the ship traveled with a doctor, there was not much he could do with a woman in labor on board—and one that was preterm as well—apart from urge the captain to get into port as soon as possible. Thankfully the ship was not far from the port of Durban, where it was due to dock later that day.

With the ship having hastened into port, the ship's captain and doctor now had more decisions to make. Should they leave my mother on board to have the baby there, or get her promptly off the ship as soon as possible to a local hospital and thus move the responsibility for my birth somewhere else? There would no doubt have been some fairly tense discussions taking place, possibly including my father, who was himself a doctor. Regardless of their deliberations, babies of course arrive on their own timetable, and I was no different. After allowing some time to pass to see if the labor was going to move along at pace, they elected to move my mother off the ship to a local hospital. Given that they were not only dealing with a mother's health but also that of a potentially medically compromised baby born too soon, it was probably a logical decision. Except that the dilly-dallying around of "move her, don't move her" meant that my arrival time had moved closer than anyone had anticipated.

My mother had been transferred onto a medical stretcher of sorts and was being wheeled to the gangway to get off the ship when things sped up. On that short trip from ship to shore, my head crowned, and I was born on the connecting jetty. A very public and, in the end, quick birth.

* * *

MY LIFE HAS BEEN one of dealing with risk, challenge, unsurety, and insecurity. It was never straightforward. However, when I think back, my parents' lives were not considered usual either; and what happened in their lives very much influenced mine.

For my father, Frenchman Philippe Latour, being a doctor was a proud generational step up for his family. His father, essentially a peasant with a basic sort of existence, knew that the way for his children to have a better life was through education. He became a grocer who would even travel to the United Kingdom in times of hardship in France to get potatoes to sell. His hard work paid off, and he was able to fund both my father, Philippe, and his brother Robert through medical school.

On the other side of the family, my mother, Louise Bennett, was British by nationality, but with parents of French descent. She lived in Mauritius as a child and later in South Africa, and I am sure would have spent time holidaying in France with the wider family. She had one sibling in her older sister, Ada, who went on to live her life on the African continent.

Before my parents married, my mother had given birth to a baby, Sylvia, fathered by someone else. Although Sylvia's birth certificate states her father as "unknown," in fact his name was Cohen; a Dutchman who was Jewish, living in South Africa at the same time as my mother. His family were closely connected with the De Beers diamond-mining interests and, as I understand it, extremely wealthy. I am not sure how old my mother would have been when they met, but I do know that his parents made it abundantly clear they did not approve of the budding romance between her and their son. They had a nice Jewish girl back in Holland in mind for him. Promptly they started making plans for their son to move there, with the aim of neatly bringing an end to the relationship with my mother. I can only imagine the sadness both he and my mother would have felt after the edict that he had to leave the country was delivered. That was how it was back then: your parents had a lot of influence on who you married. To choose to go against what they thought was best for you, or family traditions, would only be for the very brave.

As fate would have it, World War I intervened; when the war began, young Cohen was called up to serve. I am not sure of the circumstances, but soon after signing up he was killed. I am quite sure my mother would have been utterly devastated to learn of his death. She was soon to have another life-changing and stressful episode to deal with: finding out that she was pregnant. I cannot say with any certainty, but I do wonder whether the pregnancy was not a complete surprise to her, with her secretly hoping that a Cohen baby might eventuate and provide a powerful reason for them to stay together.

Planned or not, the reality of being a young, unwed mother in 1914 was not easy. Shame was piled on both mother and child. Abortion was illegal and the backstreet operations were dangerous. The only other options were adoption or foster care. Adoption as a legal entity did not exist in South Africa until 1923 and the United Kingdom until 1926, so women had to create their own arrangements—as and when they could—with couples who wanted a baby. Foster care was generally the only realistic option. A woman would pay a fee to a foster parent and, in turn, was allowed visitation rights. However, stories of malnourished children in foster care were common. Some poor women couldn't face the grim choices in front of them and took matters into their own hands. The death rate among illegitimate babies during World War I was twice that of legitimate births. The Assize Court records for the nineteenth century show that half the murder victims were babies. How sad.

My mother would have known full well that children born out of wedlock faced a shameful existence. The child she was carrying was half Jewish, too, and goodness knows what sort of extra prejudice that might bring. On top of that, "bastard" children were never able to inherit anything, and their often impoverished childhoods frequently turned into impoverished adulthoods. My mother thought that her unborn baby would be an outcast in her father's wealthy family. However, there were two things in her favor. My Aunt Ada, though secretly gay, was married. In those days, being gay or lesbian was never talked about. Homosexuality was a criminal act that you could be imprisoned for, and in South Africa prison meant hard labor. Instead it was kept very quiet and hidden in marriages. For Ada to have her sister's baby might well have served as useful evidence of a bona fide marriage. So Ada and her husband George Frieslaar, a mining inspector, could provide a stable home for Sylvia, and my mother could get on with her life knowing that her baby was safely cared for and she could still be involved in her life. It was the perfect answer to a delicate situation.

The reaction of the unborn baby's paternal grandparents to an unplanned pregnancy in the family was, perhaps, also unusual. The knowledge of a Cohen baby on the way brought with it financial support from the baby's paternal family. When Sylvia was old enough for boarding school, the Cohen family would pay for all of that, with her returning to Ada's home in the holidays.

Cohen senior was also good enough to look after my mother—not just his own bloodline. She was a milliner by vocation, and in the 1910s and 1920s hats were an integral part of a lady being well dressed; it was a good profession to be in. My mother specialized in making Panama hats and became very skilled at it. To give her security of employment, Mr. Cohen ended up buying the hat-making business my mother worked in and then gifted the entire business to her.

Things had all worked out far better for my mother than would have been usual for a single, pregnant mother at the outbreak of World War I. Her baby was looked after by her sister; she was living close by, which meant she could see her daughter grow up and be involved in her life; her child's education costs at good schools were paid for by the child's paternal grandfather; and she was the owner of a millinery business.

★ ★ ★

I AM NOT SURE what took my mother to France from South Africa, but plainly something did. As fate would have it, it was somewhere in France that she must have met and fallen in love with my father, who was a medical student at the time. They went on to get married and settle in France. Soon enough a baby was on the way—my big sister Eileen. I don't have her exact birth date, but she was three or four years older than me so she must have been born in 1917 or 1918.

Philippe's life as a doctor in France meant working in a hospital, an ongoing prospect that he felt didn't hold a lot of joy or promise for him. With a wife, a small child, and another one (me) on the way, he was keen for a fresh start. After the horrors of World War I, there was the promise of a stable, buoyant, and even flourishing 1920s stretching ahead of them like a tantalizing dream. Like many others exhausted by the grimness of the Great War, it felt like there were new horizons to investigate, new travel freedoms to take advantage of, and new lives to be explored. Being Catholic, Philippe approached the local priests with the knowledge that the Catholic Church was looking for doctors to go to the colonies to help staff the hospitals and—the other, unwritten, job of the Church—to spread the Christian faith.

The idea of going to Africa did not come completely out of the blue for my parents. It was, of course, a chance for my mother to be close to her one and only sibling, Ada, who was living in Muizenberg (a seaside suburb near Cape Town) and raising my half sister Sylvia, who by then was about six or seven years old. My father also had a cousin, Jeannine Latour, whom he was very close to, and she was already living in the Belgian Congo with her husband, Aldo, an Italian doctor, and their three sons. Philippe and Louise asked the Church if they could be stationed in the Katanga area to be close by Jeannine and Aldo, and when the answer was "yes" the move from France to Africa was sealed. My parents even chose Jeannine to be one of my godmothers before I was born—knowing that their baby would be born in Africa and grow up as part of the wider Latour family.

Although there was much to be positive and excited about in this new adventure, it was considered unwise to take a small child on the initial journey to set up their home base in a place that was very different from the stable existence they knew in France. So, it was decided that young Eileen would stay in France, to be looked after by her paternal grandparents until her parents were settled with the new baby, at which time she would join the family.

And so it was that the journey to Africa, and a new life, began for my parents. Marseille, where they left from, was a bustling city on the southeast coast of France. At the time it was the second-largest city in France, and the largest on the Mediterranean coast. Home to the country's largest commercial port, it linked the French Empire to her North African colonies of Algeria, Morocco, and Tunisia. Louise and Philippe boarded *The Grand Didier* sometime in March 1921, bound for Durban in South Africa, a journey that might have taken a couple of weeks. With both Sylvia and Eileen having arrived earlier than their due dates, my parents had factored in enough time to make the sea voyage and then take the train north to Katanga before their unborn child made an appearance. They wanted to ensure they would be well settled into their new surroundings, with Cousin Jeannine and her husband, Aldo, nearby, before I was born.

Except, it seems, I had other plans.

* * *

AS SOON AS I was born there was a huge discussion about what nation this new baby was to be attached to. Had my mother been left on board the Belgian-registered ship for just a little longer, I would have been Belgian. But because the umbilical cord was cut on South African soil, that would make me South African. There was, apparently, a lot of earnest conversation about what "rules" should apply to this unusual situation. Should I in fact be both Belgian and South African given that if I had been born a few minutes earlier it would have been on a Belgian ship in a South African port?

The French stance for a child like me born in a different country was for me to take the nationality of my French father. But to muddy things further my mother was British, and of course the British must have different rules than the French. *Their* stance was if you're born on British soil, you're British—and at the time, South Africa was a dominion within the British Commonwealth. The back-and-forth went on for quite some time before it was eventually decided that I was South African.

I have always felt the mix of nationalities and cultures that are part of my makeup. Perhaps that's not so unusual, given the tumultuous nature of the world and who controlled what countries at that time. Although my mother had spent much of her later life in South Africa, she was born in the British-controlled territory of Mauritius—an island off the southeast coast of Africa—so was considered British. British rule was in place from 1810 to 1968, when Mauritius finally became independent. Before 1810, though, Mauritius had been a French colony, so my mother's parents considered themselves French and, like many others on the island, never gave up their French passports. It was not as if becoming a British territory suddenly made the inhabitants feel British. So, my heritage is a blend of English, French, and African cultures . . . but my official nationality is South African because that was where I was born.

I would spend the first month of my life in the country of my birth, in a hospital in Durban. Since I was born two months early, it is probably remarkable that I was there for only a month; even back then I must have been a hardy survivor. I believe my mother stayed with an old school friend, either Aunt Nellie who lived in Durban opposite the Hollywoodbets Greyville Racecourse, or Nancy Cochran who lived in the suburb of Overport, some two miles away. My mother involved her close school friends in the important milestones of her life: several were her bridesmaids, and when she had children they also became godmothers. Being a godmother in those days was a serious thing, almost akin to guardianship should anything happen to the parents, so they were chosen with great care and the job accepted with equal solemnity. I imagine the support of my godmothers Nellie and Nancy was very important to my mother, with a preterm baby in the hospital and dealing with her own recovery from a less than ideal birth. My father had gone on ahead up to the Belgian Congo to start his new job alone. It must have been early May 1921 when I was deemed well enough to leave the hospital, and my mother and I headed north on a train to meet my father in the Belgian Congo and start this new chapter of our family life together.

My father had been posted to a place called Jadotville—these days known as Likasi—which was a central town surrounded by lots of mining activity in what is now the Democratic Republic of the Congo. The smaller surrounding villages were primitive, as would be expected, and the need for medical help was evident. Whether the local population wanted that help or not was debatable. At the heart of every village was a traditional healer, sometimes called a witch doctor or medicine man. These men were revered by their community, fulfilling a role that was part healer, part spiritual practitioner. They were believed to possess knowledge of herbal remedies, magic, and religious practices, so were thought to be able to treat illnesses and offer protection from evil spirits. They were also believed to have the gift of prophecy. All in all, they were important and influential members of society. These healers were leaders in their villages, able to calm or inflame disagreements with their perceived power—even pointing a bone at someone could signal death.

It seems somewhat obvious that the presence of Catholic medical doctors sent from England to "fix" the native African population was always going to create some ill-feeling—and be viewed as a threat to the power wielded by traditional healers. Africa had operated under this system of medicine for thousands of years, so it should not have been surprising that there were periods of intense unrest between the supporters of the traditional healers and the British medical staff, however well-meaning the latter were. Many in the rural African population were understandably reluctant to abandon practices that past generations had accepted. On top of which, there would have been an insistence from the traditional healers themselves that this new Western medicine was not only no good but could even be dangerous. And so the scene was set for multiple shows of strength by the healers and their supporters against the missionary workers in the hospitals and churches who were daring to suggest a new way.

My mother had only been reunited with my father for a month in their new home in the Belgian Congo when he felt the tension rising and thought it safer for me and my mother to leave for a week (or three) until things settled down again. We were bundled off in haste on a train to Bulawayo in Southern Rhodesia (now Zimbabwe) until it was considered safe to return.

By then I would have been all but two months old. My father's cousin Jeannine and her family, having been there several years, must surely have lived through a few turbulent episodes of unrest before this current flurry and would have been good support to my parents with their newborn baby. They knew, as my father had already experienced, that not all traditional healers were bad. The local healer, whom our extended Latour family knew well, was named Nyama Njoka (I have never been any good at spelling and have only ever heard his name spoken, so I think that is how it would be spelled). It is pronounced In-ya-ma In-yolk-a, which translates as "snake meat" in Swahili. *Nyama* is meat and *njoka* means snake. My family deemed Nyama, who had originated from the French Congo, to be one of the "good" ones. While other healers outwardly resented the churches and the hospitals and the people involved in them, Nyama did not, even though in reality he must have known there was a shift in power taking place.

11

We went back to Jadotville as soon as it was safe to do so. Perhaps the hope was that things would settle down again after this latest outburst; and after we returned, it did indeed seem as if life was going to plan for the next couple of months. And then it just didn't. Again, we were sent away on a rapid train ride to Bulawayo to wait for things to calm down.

However, this time the uprising was far better organized and significantly more lethal. Not long after we left, all of the hospitals and churches were attacked in one go. The "bad" healers had gathered a lot of hangers-on, and there would have ended up being about five hundred angry people. A lynch mob. They had a plan to target all of the hospitals and churches and burn them down, with all the people in them if they could.

And they were successful. My father was killed in Jadotville Hospital.

* * *

I BECAME A FOUR-MONTH-OLD baby with no father, and my mother was again a single mother—now with three children in a hugely unstable Africa.

Philippe's father immediately came out from France with my older sister Eileen to stay with my mother and me in Bulawayo. It would have been a very sad household, with everyone in it grieving the sudden loss of a son, a husband, or a father in such a shocking way.

Thankfully, Zainabu was also there. She was my African nanny, my "iya" as I called her, who would have been very helpful looking after a four-month-old and a four-year-old while a "what next" plan was being made. Zainabu had also had a parent killed at a very young age, so would have been an empathetic person for Eileen to have around. When Zainabu was a child, East Africa was a German colony and her father was German. Her mother, who was from an East African tribe, had been taken in a slave drive when Zainabu was only three. She told me later that her mother had died when a group of about thirty women, each connected to the next by a collar and a piece of wood, and with their hands and feet tied, ended up falling off a cliff. What a terrible way to go.

Zainabu's father was killed a few years later, in World War I, and she was put into a convent for orphans, where she grew up. At around the age of eighteen or nineteen she was contemplating becoming a nun when she met my father, Philippe, who had stayed at the convent very soon after arriving in Africa. The second time he visited the convent he asked if she had taken her vows yet, and when she said "no" he offered her a career change as a nanny for his newborn daughter. I am so pleased she took up his offer, because she was to become a secure and steady part of my young life.

At various stages in my life, my six godmothers all helped in my upbringing and offered me crucial support. Eileen and I called them our aunties, even though they were not related to us; Ada was the only real aunt. Aunt Dora came up from South Africa immediately after my father's death to support my mother, as did Aunt Nellie, who made the decision that her home would become our new home, too. Nellie had no children of her own and her husband, a sea captain, was away a lot; I think we became good company for her, and she had the space. She took the bottom floor and we had the top floor. It was a new chapter in my life, and I was still only four months old.

Zainabu settled locally and came daily to look after Eileen and me. Eileen was soon off to school and increasingly stayed over with Aunt Ada, so it was me who was Zainabu's primary focus. She soon moved into my bedroom overnight because a snake was found in my room. Her constant presence was comforting for me. Things settled into a new rhythm. As the sole breadwinner now, my mother's successful millinery business took up a lot of her time, with other good women rallying around to support her and her children.

We also had a good man on the scene in Pizou the cook. Like Zainabu he was of mixed ethnicity. He came from the same East African tribe as she did, but one of his parents was Chinese. Pizou and Zainabu quickly became a couple, brought together by looking after me and keeping our little household running. Romance turned into marriage, and a little granny flat was added on for the couple. We were one big family, and I certainly felt their love. I was in many ways like their child, and the first three years of my life were in a settled, loving environment. My first language was Swahili, learned from Zainabu of course. It is appropriate to say that Swahili is my "mother tongue" because she was absolutely a mother figure in my life.

My memories of my mother herself are of only seeing her at night. She was never there in the morning because she was off to work early at the hat factory, but she was there as I ended my day. Although she never read me a bedtime story, she loved singing. She taught me how to sing the first verse of "Chant du Chevalier de la Table Ronde" ("The Song of the Knight of the Round Table") and I loved singing it with her. Not that I knew this at the time, but it was a popular drinking song—those who can stay at the table for a long time are called Knights of the Round Table. To me, though, it was a marching song and we would march around to it. If you listen to it, you can hear how catchy it is. I can still remember that first verse. I can also still remember the smell of her perfume. She smelled nice, and I always knew when she was in the room because of that smell.

When I was about three, my lovely Aunt Nellie thought she was doing a good turn by offering the room in her attic to the brother of one of my other godmothers—he was a bit of a hopeless case. Never much of a worker, he was separated from his wife, whom he had only married because he'd gotten her pregnant. Their two sons, one aged two and the other only a baby, were living in my other godmother's spare room.

I did not warm to this man, and neither did Aunt Nellie. He took a shine to my mother, though. It has been written that they married and this man became my stepfather, but this is completely incorrect. It has also been written that my mother died in traumatic circumstances in his racing car. This story is also complete rubbish. Unfortunately, these tales are what this man must have told his sons and now they have become "the truth" because they have never been corrected.

The story I have read is that he was testing his car, as were other drivers, on a racetrack. When his turn came, the choke stuck or something, but—being an experienced racing driver, supposedly—he could control the car. The car was fixed overnight and the next day he drove it around the track twice with no problems. My mother then, supposedly, took a turn at driving—but when the malfunction occurred again, unlike him she couldn't control the car. It crashed, burst into flames and she was killed. *Poppycock.* Absolute rubbish. An accident like that could well have happened somewhere and sometime, but *not* to my mother in 1925. I wish I could get this story off the internet.

To make things worse, this man then registered his two sons

as the children of my now-dead mother—because by doing so he could secure them a free place in orphanage care. It was, once again, a disgraceful thing to do. I feel sorry for those boys; none of this was their fault. But I do feel that I need to set the record straight.

The truth is that my mother died of a hemorrhage. She might possibly have survived had she gotten to a hospital, but she died at the doctor's office, where she had arrived already in a serious condition. The doctor tried to get her to a hospital, but it was too late. I was three years old, maybe just four by then; I don't know exactly. And I was now both fatherless and motherless.

It was Zainabu who broke the news to me. She said to me later that I told her I was sad that I would not be able to learn the other verses of the song my mother had been teaching me. A child's way of trying to express the permanence of death, I guess.

The millinery business was inherited by Aunt Nellie and Aunt Dora. It was now time for another of my godmothers to step up and take responsibility for the next stage of my upbringing. It was decided that I would live with Jeannine Latour, my father's cousin, and her husband, Aldo the Italian doctor, in the Belgian Congo—where my parents had hoped to settle. Eileen would be the responsibility of our Aunt Ada.

Loss and picking yourself up to start again were lessons I learned early on. Thankfully, I was to start this new phase of my life with my dear Zainabu and her husband, Pizou, as my constants.

TWO

GROWING UP IN AFRICA

ONCE I HAD ARRIVED AT MY NEW HOME IN THE BELgian Congo, it was decided that I should call Aldo "Papa" and Jeannine "Tante"—French for dad and auntie. They had three sons, who were all young adults by then and living away from home for school, university, or work; it was a long time since there had been a four-year-old in the house. From memory, Gustav was sixteen, Marcel nineteen, and Leon twenty-two. I thought of them as my big brothers and loved being part of their family, which soon became *my* family. In turn, they thought of me as their little sister. I loved my inherited brothers, and I felt the love from them, too, all my life.

The boys were often away at college or working, but I would always see them when they came back to visit their parents. I remember first meeting Gustav when I had been there only a month or so. All of the brothers had beards, but he had a red one. I recall him picking me up and giving me a big hug and a kiss, and all I could do was stare at his beard. I'd never seen a red beard before. Gustav went on to train as a vet. Marcel was training to be a doctor, and would end up being a GP in Southern Rhodesia. Leon was also a doctor, off studying tropical medicine. Sadly, he would later be beheaded by the Japanese during World War II.

Zainabu and Pizou were, of course, part of the family too. They never had children and I often wondered about this, as not having children was unusual then. It was, however, a good situation for me because they were like my second parents, after Aldo and Jeannine. Tragedy having struck twice, this was a stable and loving environment for me to grow up in. I always seemed to have adults around me who cared. I was lucky in that.

I also had family close by in my Aunt Ada, who had moved up from South Africa to the Belgian Congo to be closer to me after she and her husband had divorced. When I was eight years old, Ada met her final partner, Eric Wyllie. They were a good pair, and he was a good uncle. Eric was a pilot for one of the copper-mining companies and used to take me on short trips to different mines in the plane when it suited. By the time I was twelve I could take off on my own, but he used dual control for my landings. I had a natural affinity for flying and learned quickly.

Both Sylvia and Eileen were still part of Aunt Ada's household, but they and I lived very different lives. I would hardly ever see Sylvia because she was either off at boarding school or traveling with a governess, and Eileen was away at a different boarding school in Rhodesia somewhere. Eileen did come on holidays to Aldo and Jeannine's, but usually she would spend time with Aunt Ada and Uncle Eric on the weekends. Meanwhile, my carefree childhood with Papa and Tante was to unwittingly prove to be a perfect training ground for my SOE service later in life.

Although we had a house, ours was a nomadic existence and we were hardly ever there. As one of four doctors, Papa was required to cover a huge amount of territory. Each doctor would work for two months and then have a break. Those two months were solid work, going from mine to mine, on the road all the time. We would stop at various mining areas and African villages for a few days at a time. How long we stayed depended on their size. Some of the mining townships were very small; they had no cinema or anything. Others were bustling with people. But wherever we went, it seemed, there were always people who needed to see a doctor.

Our traveling caravan consisted of five or six trucks. One was Aldo's medical truck; there were others for different staff and other support needs, a food and supplies truck, and a children's transport truck just for me. Zainabu and Pizou came too, of course, and Pizou was our cook. Zainabu would sleep with me in the nursery truck, each of us in a hammock. When we were to call into a village, we would take a buck or something similar that Pizou would butcher and cook there, and we had a milk goat that traveled with us. I was chewing biltong, a kind of jerky, from day one, I think.

Mealtimes were completely irregular; there was no pattern. We might have breakfast at 4 A.M. or 10 A.M. Some days we would go a whole day without food—friction with the tribes meant it was sometimes too dangerous to stop, so we would just keep driving. We always had plenty of food because we lived off the land—we shot it as we needed it—but I never knew when it was coming. Sometimes I would eat with the kids in the villages we stopped in, fingers and all, and would come back to the truck smelling of smoke because they had their fires inside with a little hole in the roof. Sleep was also irregular, and not always in the nursery truck. If we were staying in a village for two or three days, I would sleep in the village with the other kids.

I played happily with the African kids because I was fluent in Swahili. The monkeys were also my friends and, in reality, my only constant companions. I would chase them—where they went, I would go. I'd be up and down trees and swinging from vine to vine to follow them. Later I would find climbing and rope-wrangling a breeze in my SOE training—it was, quite literally, child's play to me. My family called me a bush baby because I was just like the African kids. Zainabu even had a pet name for me of "Baboon."

When it came to bathtime, if we came across a little spring, then I would use that to get clean. Other times, if there was enough water from rain, we would use a big drum. Pizou would fill it up halfway and I would be picked up and put in first. Zainabu would bathe second, and then others after that. When we were back at home between traveling, there was a different set of rules. I even had to wear a dress!

Although I knew that my father had died in an uprising led by traditional healers, the Latour family made sure I was introduced to our "good" local healer, Nyama Njoka, perhaps to provide some balance in my thinking. He was part of the fabric of our area. I would go and see him sometimes. He was very skinny, quite tall—unusually so at about five foot two—and mostly wore just a loincloth. Sometimes he might have worn a blanket kind of thing around his shoulders. While some healers had huts inside their village containing all sorts of mysterious items for performing their medical duties, Nyama didn't do medical things. His specialty was spells: black magic "juju" sort of stuff. He was of no fixed abode, and often slept in the bush. Different people would feed him, but maybe not enough, I think; he looked too skinny to me. Nyama told me he'd met me when I first arrived in the Belgian Congo as a newborn, while my father was still alive—not that I can remember, of course. I liked him and he must also have liked my family, I think. I did not "not believe" in what he did with spells and things, but I was also surrounded by people in the medical field who lived by science-based thought processes. Nyama seemed harmless enough to me; he sort of fascinated me.

* * *

SOME EDUCATIONAL STRUCTURE CAME into my life when I was seven. Because my family was Catholic, I was enrolled in the Catholic schooling system, through a convent. My SOE record has me at Convent de Ste. Marie-Jose in Jadotville, but I remember my schooling as being through the Institute of Saint Marie Therese and the church of that name that we sometimes attended in Jadotville. As we were hardly ever at home—and when we were it was for less than a week—I never attended the school in person. (I think in the eight years I was in the Belgian Congo, we were only ever at home for Christmas four times.) Instead I was schooled on the road by Zainabu, with the papers being sent to Belgium for marking. She was convent-educated herself and put great value on education, so kept me on track.

The curriculum covered the main theory subjects like algebra, math, geography, and history. I did not speak English, and it wasn't taught as part of my primary-age schooling. There were practical subjects, too, like botany. I remember waiting for a seed to sprout and a plant to grow. Shooting was another skill to pick up. Papa thought I should learn how to handle a gun, so that was added to my schooling. At seven we were not robust enough to manage the weight of a gun. You had to lie down and there was a fork you would put your gun in, and then off you would go, swinging the gun around to try to hit the various targets that were set up. I enjoyed it and became a pretty good shot at a young age.

There was also the option to take Morse code as a subject, but it was an extra that needed to be paid for. Papa happily signed me up, as he felt it would be a very useful thing for me to learn. He wanted me to be able to shoot a gun in the country and communicate in the city. These were useful skills for 1920s Africa. Papa knew that I would soon have the chance to go away with family members on safaris, aimed at preventing the smuggling of ivory, and I needed to know how to handle a gun so as not to be a liability on such trips. He also knew I needed to keep up with the latest technology. There were no phones in those days—timely long-distance communication was by a telegraph system operating out of a railway station or a bank. There was only one bank in Katanga, and it was always busy with people using the service—being able to communicate quickly was a growth industry. The messages would be translated into Morse code before being sent.

Morse, algebra, and math were my favorite school subjects, and I excelled at them. I really loved practicing Morse. The school had issued me with a little Morse key—a special electrical switch that you tapped—and I would click, click, click away writing messages for people to see whether they could understand them. People like Papa would then use my key and send me messages back that I would need to decode. It was fun learning a secret language that not everyone knew.

★ ★ ★

MY NEW FAMILY WAS good for me, though my birth parents were never lost to me. Papa and Tante kept them alive through talking about them and having photos of them around. I would kiss the photos good morning, kiss the photos goodbye, kiss the photos goodnight. If something exciting happened, I'd rush to my parents' photos and tell them all about it. I know I once got smacked by Papa for doing something wrong, and I went and told them all about that, too.

I must have been about six when I discovered I had not been adopted by Papa and Tante. I was terribly upset. I thought it meant they didn't really want me. They sat me down and explained that my parents would always be my parents. Papa and Tante were my guardians, "substitute parents," who would do anything a parent would and loved me just as a birth parent would. When, as an adult, I thought back on this, I thought it was sensible of them really. It gave me something that was mine and mine only: my parents.

Tragedy would continue to follow me, though. At seven, our formal convent education came with the religious aspect as well, which included first communion. It was a big event in our family. I wore a beautiful little white dress, and Papa, Tante, and everyone made a big fuss of me. It would be the last family occasion Tante would see. She died about a month later when she was out alone on a horse ride.

She had been thrown by her horse after it stood on a puff adder snake, which then bit her. The flustered horse found its way back to the house on its own. A riderless horse was never a good thing to see. The staff did not know which bridle path Tante had taken, so unfortunately it took some time to find her, and by the time they did she was dead. The venom from a puff adder bite can be

23

lethal unless the victim can get antivenom treatment quickly. We were away traveling that day and came straight home to Jadotville on hearing the news. I remember seeing Tante laid out at the family home—she had turned a blue color. At her funeral there was much talk about how wonderful it was that she had been alive for my first communion. It seemed a strange thing to be happy about. The God I had just pledged my commitment to in a big ceremony full of pomp and circumstance was the same God who could take Tante away from us.

Aldo was devastated. He went very silent after that; the old Papa I knew had gone. He didn't attend any more church ceremonies or the like, either. Maybe he was thinking the same thing I was about the cruelty of God. Thankfully, the next few years passed without the loss of any more important people in my life. I began to travel farther afield. My birth father's father took me to Italy and Germany for seven months of the year when I was about eight, and to France for nine months or so when I was ten. We visited relatives in Lyon; I am not sure, but I think that was where my father, Philippe, was born. These trips opened my eyes to the world outside Africa, polished up my French, and gave me an ear for other European languages, namely Italian and German.

Once I turned eleven, Papa knew that things needed to change if I was to make my way in the world. He thought it best for me to move to a bigger, city-based school for my teenage years. I would take exams at age fifteen, and it was important to do well in these. A good result would mean a ticket to England to finish my education. Papa was aware that my English was not good and that it would be crucial when the time came to take the exams, so he looked for an interim solution for me for a year, during which I could learn

English. Trouble also seemed to be brewing again with local communities, and Papa felt it would be safer for me to be far away from the growing tension.

I would be going to Kenya.

When Papa broke the news of his intended plan, I was of course very sad. I loved the Belgian Congo, the people in it, and the freedom it afforded me. Before I left, I went to visit our Nyama to tell him I was going. He said he would make sure I was safe until I could return. After producing a monkey's foot and performing a small ceremony over it, he put it in a little sack (probably made of another animal part). Handing it to me, he told me earnestly that it would keep me safe wherever I traveled. I had no idea whether the spell he had put on it would work or not, but I accepted it gratefully. As I packed this symbolic piece of my childhood in my bag, it dawned on me that I had no idea when—or even if—I would be back in the Belgian Congo to see his toothless grin and all that I loved about this place. I fervently hoped I *would* be back one day.

★ ★ ★

IT WAS WITH A heavy heart that I left my beloved home in the Belgian Congo. Although I knew Papa was only doing what he thought was best for me, it was difficult to leave so much that was familiar. I never wanted to grow up, and it felt as if life was forcing me to do just that. I was still only twelve years old.

I am not sure how the school in Kenya was selected, but it was a good choice for me—it was not too structured—and I lived in a family home. Jock and June Henderson, an English couple who lived on a coffee farm close to Nyeri at the foot of Mt. Kenya, had two children, and the work-around to not sending them away to school was to start a school themselves. I don't recall the name of the school, but I do know it was the name of their home. The Hendersons took in six pupils, me included, to make it a bona fide place of education. Three of us were about twelve years old; the rest were a bit younger.

All of us needed to learn English properly. This included the Henderson children, because they spent most of their time with the local African families, just like I had in the Belgian Congo. At this stage I was fluent in the languages that were all around me: Walloon, a language spoken in some parts of Belgium and related to French; Flemish (the Dutch spoken in other parts of Belgium); French; and Patwa (or patois), a mixture of all the languages together. And, of course, Swahili. I could also speak well enough to get by in Kikuyu, the second-most-dominant language in Kenya.

But I did not speak English—I might know a few words here and there, but I did not know the language. So, the key focus of this school year was to learn to read, write, and speak the English language correctly. The writing I found hard; even now, don't ask me to spell anything—my spelling has never really improved.

The house was on a large coffee plantation, and I loved the freedom of seeing the wide-open spaces around me. The lush green of the coffee plants, the deep red of the earth, and the blue of the Aberdare mountains in the distance were good for my soul. I missed Papa, Zainabu, and Pizou enormously—but if I couldn't be back there, then this place suited me as a good second-best. I even learned to ride a horse and very quickly came to love the gentle natures of these animals. Papa had chosen well.

Sadly, though, things could not stay this way forever. With my

English much improved by year-end, the next piece of my education jigsaw lay ninety-three miles away in big, bustling Nairobi. The Nairobi European School (later renamed The Kenya High School) was everything my time in Nyeri was not. The only good thing that came out of that place was Barbara Smithson, a fellow boarder who was the one good friend I made; she would one day become my bridesmaid.

I was utterly miserable. I had gone from a home-boarding situation to a big dormitory, a relaxed home-based learning environment to a strict one in a classroom, and magnificent countryside out the front door to a less-than-attractive city. Back at the coffee farm, if I had wanted breakfast at four o'clock in the morning, I could make it myself. But The Nairobi European School had rules, like any boarding school does. They were rigid. I had to eat and sleep when they said; and the teaching was in a classroom, which I didn't like. It didn't suit me. I counted down the days to when I could be released to the care of Aunt Ada. At the very start of my time there, she was living in the Belgian Congo—and with it being so far away, that meant only seeing her on holidays. Thankfully, Ada soon moved much closer, along with her partner, Eric, so I could go there on the weekends. This made life much more bearable.

* * *

ALTHOUGH I LIKE TO think that my being at school so far away might have had a bearing on their decision, Aunt Ada and Eric had decided to move to Kenya when unrest began brewing in the Belgian Congo again. In previous uprisings, I believe, there were orders from the Belgians not to kill any of the traditional healers, reinforcing the belief these men put about that bullets couldn't kill them. This time, though, the Belgians wanted to show the healers' followers that they did not, in fact, possess any magical, godlike powers, and so a few were killed to prove this point. Eric and Ada knew it was time to leave—in their opinion, the unrest was only going to get worse.

Eric left his job as a pilot for the mining company and they found a lovely piece of land in what was then a brand-new suburb called Lang'ata, in Nairobi. In the 1930s Nairobi was a growing colonial city, and Lang'ata was known for its open spaces with large estates and farms that were being established. Eric and Ada made the move for the long term, intending to make their future livelihood as gamekeepers and safari guides with big game on the Serengeti.

The move came with another decision—to get married. I had always thought that they *were* married, so the announcement of their impending nuptials was a bit of a surprise to me. Eric, some ten years younger than Ada, became husband number four. And it was "fourth time lucky" for Aunt Ada, because that marriage was her last, and the longest at thirty-odd years' duration. Eric had always taken an interest in me, and I liked him in return. Their wedding, during my first year at The Nairobi European School, was a highlight of happiness for me in what was otherwise a year I just wanted to be over. My older half sister Sylvia also got married—a week later—to a chap from Rhodesia called Ernest Watkins. Things finally seemed to be settling down around me.

My escapes to Ada and Eric's home on the weekends and for term breaks kept me going through my final years of schooling. There it was that my love for the wide-open Serengeti plains and the graceful animal life that dwelled there was ingrained in me.

It was my happy place in which to sit and absorb the beauty of the majestic landscape. Outside the front door there was game everywhere—leopards, lions, all sorts of things. I would lie awake at night listening to hyenas hunting for food. We had a *boma* (enclosure) surrounding the house to protect our livestock from the predators roaming the vast plains. I was even able to rear a cheetah cub as a hunting companion. Eric realized that I was a good shot, and hence could be a good hunter, so would take me out on the Serengeti to hone my skills.

Ada and Eric also started breeding Rhodesian ridgebacks and German shepherds—good guard dogs. I loved being around the dogs, my cheetah, and the amazing wildlife that surrounded me. I just loved the animals and the wide-open spaces of Africa. It was good for my soul, and a salve for the education at The Nairobi European School, which I found relentless.

* * *

AT AGE FIFTEEN, THE time came for "the" test at the end of the school year. The Junior Cambridge test from the University of Cambridge in England unlocked the all-important next phase of education, and I was aware of its significance. How could I not be? It was the main reason why Papa and Aunt Ada had sent me away to boarding school—so that I could do well enough in this exam. Passing it would give me a choice: I could move to England for the next stage of my education or stay in Africa. Personally, I hoped to stay in Africa. England held no appeal for me; I knew nothing of it.

When the day came, I felt pretty confident. Both Papa and Aunt Ada had warned me that I might struggle with the spelling, but I was very good at other things so I felt that on balance I would pass. My best subject was mathematics, and in the tests my lowest score was 82 percent; I even got 100 percent on one of them. I loved numbers and patterns, and having learned Morse code and algebra from the age of seven, it was not hard for me to do well.

Then there was the dictation test. I listened hard to the teacher who was telling me what I needed to spell. "Spell laugh," she said, with a face that had no humor about it. The girls around me quickly wrote their answers on their exam paper. I knew this was a bit of a trick one because while it was sensible to spell it with an "f," I knew it ended in "gh." The teacher repeated the request: "Spell laugh." I thought of Ada's second husband, George Frieslaar. "Laa" had the same sound as laugh. Now, I also spoke a bit of Afrikaans, a kind of Dutch, and in that language words with a short-sounding "a" would only have one "a." Therefore, it seemed logical that a word like "laugh" would have two "a"s, like Freislaar did. I wrote "laaugh." The teacher continued down her list. "Spell laughing." I wrote laaughing. Logical. "Spell laughter." I quickly wrote down laaughter.

In the dictation test you were allowed two mistakes; I had twenty. Regardless of my exemplary math scores, the poor spelling results meant that I failed Junior Cambridge in its entirety. I hated the British and their silly education system.

Now there were decisions to be made about my schooling. I always knew that the intended schooling path was England, because Africa did not provide the education that Papa and Aunt Ada thought suitable at this stage of my life. But if I was not to go to England (not that I'd ever wanted to and certainly did not now), what might my choices be?

Aunt Ada and Papa conferred with the extended family. The decision that was eventually delivered to me was not one I had thought was even a possibility. It was an offer from a school run by another of my godmothers, Josianne. It seems that it was her turn to help bring up an orphan. I knew of Josianne's existence, but only in name. I am not sure how she was connected to me—she might have been a distant cousin of my father's or someone my mother knew through her schooling—but I did not question this. My other godmothers had gotten involved in my life when I needed someone to look after me, so I presumed that Josianne would be as reliable as the rest.

Josianne lived in Paris and ran a small finishing school for just twelve students out of her home in Montparnasse. She had space for one more pupil on the roll. I could live at the school three days a week, and Josianne's father would house me for the rest of the week. This sort of schooling would normally be off-limits given the cost, but as I was Josianne's goddaughter it must have come at the right price, which must have been free. It was deemed the best plan for me for the next three years. I would polish up my English, learn French, and be exposed to the arts and literature scene of Paris—perhaps readying me to become a suitable bride one day.

By the time I finished my education at age eighteen it would be diverse—bush baby in the Belgian Congo, free spirit in the outdoors of the Serengeti, classroom-contained in Kenya, and finished off in Paris. It was an eclectic mix.

THREE

EUROPE AND THE START OF WAR

MY NEW LIFE IN PARIS WAS COMPLETELY UNLIKE LIFE in Kenya. Montparnasse, where L'école des Jeunes Filles (The School for Young Ladies) was run by my godmother Josianne, was an arty sort of district in the fourteenth arrondissement of Paris on the left bank of the River Seine. The area had become famous in the 1920s and 1930s as the heart of intellectual and artistic life in Paris, so it was the perfect place for Josianne to mold her students into educated young ladies.

Apart from me—the girl from Africa and the goddaughter of the school's owner—there were a couple of English girls, and the rest of the twelve students were Swiss. The main language in Switzerland at the time was German, and so for these young women to learn French properly (for families who felt that was important), the best way to do it was to go to school in Paris to "finish" your education at finishing school. The classroom was the lounge, and we would gather there to talk about a variety of educative subjects—history,

33

geography, the arts—and refine our (Parisian) French. There were also lessons in etiquette and deportment. Walking across the room with a book on your head was indeed a thing.

My four-day weekend was spent with Josianne's father, André Doman, whom I called Grandfather. Of course he was not my grandfather, but Josianne had said that they both thought it a nice idea to do that because he would be like one to me. So I did, and he was. I liked him instantly. I think he must have been widowed and might have been a bit lonely; maybe I was his new project. Grandfather took it upon himself to continue my education in the days I stayed with him by visiting the many beautiful places in Paris. We would regularly visit the Louvre and other museums. If the intention of Papa, Ada, Grandfather, and Josianne was to make me a lady and finish my education "properly" with a nice Parisian accent, it was all falling into place. The Parisian accent maybe not so much. As much as Josianne tried to change the way I pronounced my "r"s, it had little effect. I continued to speak French with a Flemish accent, as I had from childhood.

In my first year in Paris—1937—Grandfather lived in the area around Avenue Foch, close by the Arc de Triomphe. Little did we know then that Avenue Foch would become a feared address in just a few years' time, when the city became occupied by the Nazis. Number 84 Avenue Foch in particular—that building became the Gestapo headquarters and the site of torture for captured agents like Violette Szabo of SOE and members of the French Resistance. In hindsight, it was almost as if I was being gifted a look at Paris before things turned ugly. The ugliness was not far away, though. Hitler's goal of dominance in Europe was making the Continent increasingly unstable. After the Nazi regime took power in 1933, Germany began working toward rearmament—forbidden under the Treaty of Versailles signed after World War I—and in 1936 remilitarized the Rhineland, which bordered France. This signaled a change in the balance of European power from France and its allies toward Germany.

Although I could feel a sense of rising tension, there was of course nothing I personally could do about it. I was in fact enjoying living and learning in Paris after the misery of high school in Kenya. Before the end of the first school year, Grandfather moved to Montparnasse to be closer to his daughter, which meant less travel for me. One of my most favorite activities was walking with him around le Jardin du Luxembourg, which was not far away.

Following World War I, Paris had witnessed an unprecedented festive and artistic proliferation, and even though the Great Depression had pulled life back into the gray, a strong bohemian presence remained in the Montparnasse area. This was reflected in the cafés and brasseries of the district, especially in some of the more celebrated establishments like La Coupole on the Boulevard du Montparnasse in the fourteenth arrondissement. Opened in 1927 in the Roaring Twenties to great fanfare, and frequented by painters, sculptors, actors, and journalists, it soon exuded 1930s deco style from every corner. It was quintessential arty Paris.

La Coupole was a favorite haunt of Grandfather's, and he would often take me there. It was all part of my Parisian education. I very quickly became on first-name terms with the man who ran it—Ivan. I do not even know his last name; he was just Ivan to me. He and Grandfather would often talk, sometimes with others, too, about everything from the local goings-on to the wider world picture. I sat and absorbed it all.

35

When war broke out, La Coupole became a place the French Resistance met and a known safe house in Paris for SOE. My sixteen-year-old self, sitting there in 1937 with my adopted grandfather in a peaceful Paris, could never have imagined that a world war was just a couple of years away; or what being in Paris, in this very building, would mean for me later as a secret agent with SOE.

★ ★ ★

THE YEAR 1938 WAS very different from 1937, as the winds of change came sweeping through Europe. Hitler annexed Austria in March that year, and on Grandfather's regular visits to the school in the following days I heard much discussion between him and Josianne about Hitler's aggression. Grandfather was a World War I veteran—a general, no less—so he felt keenly the fragility of peace. "Josianne, mark my words—Czechoslovakia will be next," I would hear him warn. "We must be prepared."

I wasn't sure what preparation would mean in real terms, but presumed that when Grandfather signaled me to leave the room with a wave of his hand, that "preparation" was what he and Josianne were discussing. He had a constant look of worry about him. Our carefree visits to the Louvre, walks in the gardens, and joviality at La Coupole seemed a distant memory.

World War I was not something Grandfather liked to talk about, and it was not something I would ever have brought up myself. But having fought in that war some twenty years earlier, he was plainly concerned about the instability of Europe. Hitler was now making inflammatory speeches about the need for Germans in Czechoslovakia to be reunited with their homeland. I would often hear

Grandfather talk with his daughter about the hard-fought-for wins of the Great War and how there should never be another war like that.

"Czechoslovakia is independent," he would insist. "The war saw to that; we can't go backward. We said we would help them if this ever happened—and now we say we cannot."

Josianne would nod her head fervently in agreement, adding comments that made me quietly think that war was inevitable. "Papa," she would say, a tone of resignation evident in her voice, "we must prepare for the worst if help does not come."

I wondered what "help" would come to Czechoslovakia, if any. The newspapers had been full of conjecture about whether France or Britain would go to Czechoslovakia's defense, but both of these countries had now deemed that they were not obliged to do so. The memory of the Great War was so very fresh in everyone's minds; nobody wanted another military confrontation with Germany so soon. I found myself wondering whether Grandfather would be called up if a second world war broke out, given his senior army rank in the Great War. I fervently hoped he would be deemed too old, and that things would settle down. But alas, they did not.

Hitler's speeches were reported in the newspapers and, as the year wore on, Grandfather would pore over each one, reading pieces aloud to his daughter and then taking a step back from the paper on the table, as if physically distancing himself from the words would somehow make them less disturbing. With Hitler laying claim to Sudetenland, a region of Czechoslovakia with a substantial ethnic German population, peace in Europe was now clearly at risk.

Radio was the newest form of communication available to us. Hearing Hitler himself utter the words of his speeches was even more shocking than seeing them in print. Grandfather and Josianne would sit close to the radio, absorbing the words and what they meant.

Hitler's September 26, 1938, speech demanding the Sudetenland region of Czechoslovakia finally shone a light on the dark fears that Grandfather had harbored.

We don't want the Czechs. Our demand for the Sudetens is irrevo-cable. Beneš [Edvard Beneš, the president of Czechoslovakia] can choose peace or war. He will either accept my demands, or I will go to liberate the Germans.

I am the first soldier. Let the world know that behind me the people march in step. Let the world know it is a different people from 1918.

The current state of things also became part of our conversations at school. It was hard to ignore. Josianne continued to put on a brave face for her students, but we all knew she was preoccupied. Just a few days later, Grandfather and Josianne were again listening to the radio. I felt I should keep my distance to let father and daughter di-gest the next grim chapter of this story, but this time the broadcast was full of the sounds of jubilant crowds. Without asking, I joined them in the sitting room where they were huddled by the radio.

"War might be avoided," Grandfather said as he smiled at me. "You know, I think there's still hope—they have gotten together in Munich to find a way." He patted the seat next to him, signaling me to come and listen to what was being said.

The British prime minister, Neville Chamberlain, was speaking to the assembled press in Britain. Fresh from his meeting the previ-

ous day with Hitler, a relatively new French premier Édouard Da-
ladier, and the Italian dictator Benito Mussolini, he was reading the
understanding they had come to.

> We regard the agreement signed last night and the Anglo-German
> Naval Agreement as symbolic of the desire of our two peoples never
> to go to war with one another again.
>
> We are resolved that the method of consultation shall be the
> method adopted to deal with any other questions that may concern
> our two countries, and we are determined to continue our efforts to
> remove possible sources of difference, and thus to contribute to assure
> the peace of Europe.

This was the famous Munich Agreement, which permitted Nazi
Germany to annex Sudetenland in the hope that this would be a
diplomatic solution that would curb a wider war in Europe. Outside
number 10 Downing Street later that day, Chamberlain would go
on to tell the public that he had returned from Germany bringing
peace with honor. "I believe it is peace for our time," he said, before
suggesting that people "go home and get a nice quiet sleep." To
my seventeen-year-old mind this seemed like a seminal moment,
but I looked to Grandfather—wise, war-weary, and war-wary—for
his reaction. His expression was now hard to read, and I wondered
whether he was simply too scared to believe there was a real possibility of averting war. To have survived the horrors of the Great
War and to now be on the brink of a second world conflict must
have been terrible to contemplate.

He was not the only one with doubts. A man whose name I
would come to know all too well was soon taking the contrary view.

British Conservative minister of parliament Winston Churchill decried Chamberlain's appeasement of Hitler, telling him he had been given the choice between war and dishonor and that "you chose dishonor, and you will have war."

He would, sadly, be proven right; but perhaps at that moment, that day in Montparnasse, we chose not to think of that sobering possibility.

★ ★ ★

ANOTHER YEAR ROLLED OVER, another winter passed; as the end of the school year came closer, I could see in Josianne a rising sense of anxiety. Her concerns were now plainly evident. And it wasn't just her—I saw that same anxiety etched into the faces of the people on the Parisian streets and heard it in the conversations at La Coupole. Although summer was on the way, there was a chill in the air in more ways than one. In May 1939 the level of anxiety was increased with the signing of a "Pact of Friendship and Alliance" between Germany and Italy. Hitler and Mussolini formally in lockstep with one another was ominous and raised the question of what next.

Sure enough, one day in June, instead of the usual talk of "les grandes vacances" coming up with the summer break not far away, Josianne said she had something important to tell us.

"Ladies, we have seen the fall of Austria, the annexation of the Sudetenland, the fall of Czechoslovakia, and threats against Poland. France may well be next. This school is no longer a safe place for you to be."

We girls had all read the signals from Josianne that things were changing, so it did not really come as a surprise when she said the school would be closing because of the imminent threat of war. We were all to finish the school year as planned in the next couple of weeks, but classes would not reopen in the autumn.

Most of the girls went home to (neutral) Switzerland as soon as travel arrangements could be made; eventually I was the only student left. Was it to be Africa for me, I wondered. Might this cosmopolitan Parisian life soon be exchanged for the open plains of the Serengeti, a place I loved? Or would it be England? I knew there would be a discussion between Grandfather and Josianne in the coming days about the next chapter of my life. This did not worry me; I had become accustomed to change.

Once again, the wider family had been consulted, and between Papa, Aunt Ada, Josianne, and Grandfather a plan had come together. Josianne sat me down and came straight out with it.

"Grandfather and I have been thinking about the best way to keep you safe. We have spoken with your family in Africa, and we think you should make for Spain."

I must have looked somewhat surprised, but before I could say anything she explained the decision.

"Spain is neutral, and it borders Gibraltar—a British territory. So if Spain came into the war, you could move south to Gibraltar and from there get yourself to England."

It was clear that the adults around me—who wanted the best for me—had already thought this through. Who was I to question their wisdom? I simply accepted this as the plan. Besides, I did not like the thought of going to England. I didn't really like the English, and England was as likely to be in the firing line as France, so I could see why Spain was a safer option. Except that I knew no one there.

Within days my life was on the move again—quite literally. I was about to pack a small bag for the journey when Josianne came into my room.

"You won't be needing a bag," she said. "You will be walking into Spain and that means not taking anything with you."

She must have read the confusion and concern on my face, as she continued: "It is just while you get there. It is easier this way. You will have money to buy clothes and whatever else you need once you get over the mountains."

No clothes, no knowledge of Spanish, and walking over the Pyrénées. These things all seemed to be of little concern to the people close to me. Maybe any doubts they had remained unvoiced, but either way I did not feel I could say anything. I knew I could pick up Spanish easily enough because, like French, it was in the family of Romance languages, so I would soon have enough to get by. I felt confident that I could be fluent within a month or two.

For most of my life I had lived through constant change, so deep down I knew I was capable of rising to the challenge. In any case, it felt like there was no choice.

★ ★ ★

THE FAREWELLS WERE HARD. But over the years I had done a fair few of those, too, so I just got on with it and swallowed any feelings of sadness and nervousness as best I could. Josianne and my beloved Grandfather bade me farewell on the platform at the Montparnasse train station, handing me over to Marcel Luchard, a young Flemish man. He was charged with getting not only me to Spain, but also a Jewish couple. As I boarded the train for Toulouse, and we settled into seats together, I looked at my fellow travelers and wondered what was in store for us. I knew it was going to be an arduous journey with no guarantee of success.

From Toulouse, we took a bus to a small town a couple of hours away. A few minutes of walking behind Marcel saw us arrive at a house on the edge of town, where I gratefully ate the food offered and fell into a deep slumber after what had been a very long day. The next day, another traveler joined our party—a young Frenchman, perhaps in his twenties. Now a walking party of five, we headed off into the rural landscape. As the day drew to a close, we stopped outside a farmhouse selected by Marcel. Reaching into his pocket of cash and peeling off a few notes, he went in to see if we could pay them for a meal and a bed for the night. This was our daily routine for some two or three weeks as we crisscrossed from town to town through the lowlands, waiting to get the word that we could make the attempt to climb up and over the Pyrénées to Spain.

Sometimes we were lucky, and a farmer would have a horse and cart that would make the trek to the next abode quicker. There was increasing competition for places to sleep as we encountered more and more groups of people also trying to walk out of France. While we might be competing for resources, we would always exchange a look of empathy. We were all in the same boat—waiting until we could make for the hills and attempt to cross into Spain undetected. Thankfully, it was July and the height of summer—this was not something you would want to attempt in cold weather.

However, we were not to be successful. We never got to stay at the house that had the front door in France and the back door in Spain. At the most recent place we were staying—very close to what our guide thought would be the best crossing—the farmer laid the reality out for us over the evening meal.

"The border is too well guarded," he told us. "Guards are every-where," he warned, "and so are the dogs."

Getting through the border was not the end of it, either. If you slipped through undetected but were then caught in Spain, you would be sent back to France. If you were less lucky, you could end up in Miranda de Ebro—a detention camp.

The reality of what might happen in Spain had, of course, not been explained to me; the plan had been to just take things as they came. Josianne and Grandfather obviously had great faith in my ability—at eighteen—to fend for myself.

Our walking group slept on the information, and when we left the house the next morning it was not to press forward to Spain but to turn back into France. Marcel told us this would be wise. As with the other big life decisions made on my behalf, I accepted his counsel. I was, in fact, quietly relieved.

Marcel would get the whole party back to the town where the young Frenchman had joined us, and from there we would go our own ways. He did, though, undertake to return me to Paris. Be-cause the route was pretty much a straight line back through the lowlands, rather than zigzagging from place to place to place, he thought the return journey would take us less than a week.

By this time, though, Marcel had almost run out of the stash of notes that Josianne (on my behalf) and the rest of our group had given him to pay for his guiding duties. At the first house we stopped at—one we had stayed in before—I could see that he was haggling with the owner, and the farmer waved him away. He had more than enough customers; there was no reason to accept anything but the going rate. At the second house it was the same, but this time Marcel reluctantly paid the same rate as when we had stayed there all of a week or so ago. We were once again fed and watered for the night and had a place to sleep.

Marcel must have gotten up very early the next morning, as I saw him coming back to the house as I was ready to leave.

"We need to get on the road now," he said, and I could see why. He had a bag of food hidden under his coat and some extra cash rolled up in his pocket; he must have stolen these from the occupants of another house nearby. We walked a long way that day, and the next, with Marcel's light-fingered ways helping to get us fed and rested enough for another long walk.

Little did I know that walking for days and days on end, with no access to regular food and having no roof over my head, would become my new normal in five years' time in another part of France. This was an easy version of what I would have to deal with, but at the time I felt a quiet anxiety. I was certainly pleased to get to Toulouse and board the train for Paris with Marcel. I had been away a month.

* * *

BEING BACK IN MONTPARNASSE was like putting on a comfortable pair of shoes. Josianne was relieved to see me back; I think that the hastily thought-out plan not working was a blessing to her and to Grandfather. But I knew it would only be a temporary stay. France was a ticking bomb with war about to break out. There would be another plan; I just didn't know what it was yet. A few days after I got back home, late in August 1939, I heard Josianne talking to a visitor about a piece in the news they had both read the day before.

"What do you make of it?" she asked in an earnest tone.

"It is unbelievable, not true. Or could it be hopeful?" he answered.

Neither of them looked remotely hopeful, however. After Hitler's promises the previous year to just take Sudetenland, he had gone on to annex the remainder of Czechoslovakia a few months later. Hitler's promises were worth nothing, so another announcement about a peaceful way forward was met with no expectations.

The previous day, Grandfather had called to see Josianne, as he so regularly did. I loved their routine and being a part of it again. I sat with them as they had their usual hot drinks together and listened to the radio. The man reading the news had a certain edge to his voice that I usually didn't hear; it prompted me to listen more closely.

"Germany and the Soviet Union have agreed to a pact of non-aggression. The surprising announcement was made in Berlin last night by the official German news agency. Early this morning the Russian Tass Agency issued a similar statement."

Grandfather and Josianne's reaction was one of bemusement. A pact between Hitler and Stalin, who hated each other, seemed utterly implausible. Hitler had always said that the Soviet Union was his enemy, claiming it was ruled by Jewish communists and subhuman Slavs. Even more improbably, this nonaggression pact, signed on August 23, 1939, pledged that they would not attack each other for ten years! It was, of course, too good to be true. History would show that less than two years later, in June 1941, Hitler would launch an invasion of the Soviet Union in Operation Barbarossa. The man was not to be trusted.

The pact was also, of course, a disaster for Poland, and what happened next saw the start of World War II. The secret parts of the agreement allowed Germany to invade Poland—which happened just a week later, on September 1. France and Britain declared war two days later, but it would take them months to fully mobilize their armies. On September 17, Poland found itself fighting a war on two fronts when the Soviet Union invaded from the east.

Following heavy shelling and bombing, Warsaw officially surrendered to the Germans on September 28. In accordance with the secret protocol in their nonaggression pact, Germany and the Soviet Union partitioned Poland the very next day.

FOUR

TO BRITAIN AND
WAR WORK

THE TIMES WE'D SPENT BY THE RADIO LISTENING TO the news in late August had been somber. The hot drinks we'd poured before sitting down to listen often sat unfinished, perhaps as hard to swallow as the news. War in Europe was coming. I knew that this meant things would happen in a hurry for me, and they certainly did.

The ridiculous nonaggression pact between Germany and the Soviet Union was the last straw. Josianne and Grandfather sent me off to England as soon as they could, and this time I could pack a small bag. I snuck in Nyama Njoka's monkey-foot charm from my childhood to keep me safe. Even if it was all nonsense, it was nice to have as a reminder of my carefree days in the Belgian Congo. Who knows, maybe it was indeed magic? If it was, it was divine protection that I wanted on my side.

Like my parents eighteen years before, I found myself at the port of Marseille boarding a passenger ship. But unlike them, I was not off to beloved Africa on a long-planned journey. I was among a crush of people all hurriedly trying to leave France on the last peacetime passenger ships. Mine was bound for Liverpool. Despite me having no affinity with England, once again I accepted the decision of my elders.

It was harder to say goodbye to Grandfather this time. He seemed such an old man now—I did not know when, or if, I would see him again. He felt bony and a bit fragile when I hugged him and breathed in his familiar scent. I hoped I would smell that smell again and feel his arms around me sometime in the future. "You're okay, my girl, off you go. Don't worry about me," he said. I drew strength from his positivity, but couldn't help feeling uncertain inside as I waved him goodbye in Paris.

My farewell to Josianne in Marseille, following a long train trip, was also difficult. She spoke positively: "Lucky we got you on this ship, Pippa. It was meant to be." This was followed by a big hug and a kiss on my forehead, like a mother with a small child—except that we were both grown women. When she teared up, I felt a welling inside me, too.

"Off you go—they need you on board now," she instructed, pointing me toward the gangplank. I walked up it, with the many others crowding onto the ship out of France—their ticket out of an impending war zone—and chose not to look back in case it made me feel even worse. Others did look back; suddenly I seemed to be surrounded by wailing women and children.

The trip from Marseille began on the flat seas of the Mediterranean in balmy weather, followed by battling the strong tidal currents of the Strait of Gibraltar between Morocco and the Iberian Peninsula—only a bit over eight miles across at its narrowest point—

and ended with typically gloomy English weather in Liverpool. It was only meant to take a few days, but at one point in the journey we had to duck into a port briefly when a submarine was reported close by. It turned out to be a false sighting, but it was indicative of the nervous state everyone was in.

In England I would initially be staying with the Wyllie family in Portsmouth, a seaport in southern England. This was where Aunt Ada's husband Eric's family was from. Harold, Uncle Eric's older brother (whom I would soon call Uncle Harold), was there to meet me when the ship docked, and we took the train back to Portsmouth. Harold was the oldest of nine children born to the renowned maritime artist William Lionel Wyllie, whose work can still be found in prestigious galleries around the world. Wyllie senior had died some eight years previously. He had spent his later years at Tower House—the house I was to stay at, built right on the edge of the harbor. It was a dream house for a maritime artist, with a great view; and quite the place for me to live for a few weeks while we sorted out what would come next for me.

Soon, I was enrolled at a place that taught shorthand and typing. I couldn't stand the typing. We had to type to music—it really wasn't me. I moved into a room at the YWCA in the Portsmouth suburb of Southsea. It came with breakfast and high tea for "two and six" (two shillings and sixpence) a fortnight, and was my first step into independent adulthood. I needed more than the meager clothing I had brought with me to look even semipresentable, so I found a few pieces that did the job at the local Salvation Army shop.

* * *

WITHIN A FEW MONTHS, the war began gearing up. Portsmouth harbor had been chained off to stop submarines, and there was talk of Portsmouth itself being a bombing target. Germany was on the move, advancing rapidly through Luxembourg, the Netherlands, Belgium, and France. Toward the end of May 1940, mostly British, many French, and some Belgian soldiers were trapped by the German army in a small area around Dunkirk in northern France. Evacuation by sea was the only option, but looked extremely challenging.

However, Operation Dynamo, which occurred between May 26, and June 4, did the miraculous. The amphibious rescue utilized all manner of seafaring vessels, from large Navy ships to minute civilian boats, to help the troops escape to England while under German attack. With so many of their troops rescued, the British Army could regroup to fight another day.

Paris was taken on June 14, 1940, and by the 22nd the French had surrendered to the Germans. The terms of the Armistice allowed the southern half of France to remain under French civil administration, with the new French government (essentially a puppet state of Germany) based in Vichy in central France. Northern France was occupied by the Germans. (By late 1942 the Germans and Italians would occupy the whole of France, but in June 1940 a demarcation line was drawn between the occupied and "free" zones.)

Refusing to accept his government's 1940 armistice with Germany, General Charles de Gaulle fled to England, and encouraged the French to continue the fight from afar. Winston Churchill, by now British prime minister, was faced with a terrible dilemma. He could either trust the French government to keep their promise not to hand over their ships to Hitler, or he could make the problem go away by destroying the ships himself. In early July 1940 he did the latter, and sank those ships of the French fleet that were not berthed in the safety of an English port. The attack, called Operation Catapult, took place off the coast of North Africa on July 3. Churchill later wrote: "This was the most hateful decision, the most unnatural and painful in which I have ever been concerned."

By late June 1940, Uncle Harold and I both knew that the war was now concerningly close, with only the English Channel between us and the enemy. Uncle Harold had connections in the Navy, and with the Admiralty moving their administrative facility northward up to Scotland, he thought that would be a far safer place for me than Portsmouth. And so another chapter of my life began.

★ ★ ★

THE ADMIRALTY OPERATION RAN out of Ardencaple Castle on the River Clyde near Helensburgh, just north of Glasgow, the gracious old building having been requisitioned by the Royal Navy. I was working under British scientist Henry Hulme, then head of the Degaussing Department, which was looking at how to stop magnetized mines sticking to the iron hulls of ships. I was in Records—a kind of library—and it was my job to know where every ship was and provide information about it when asked. It was a job that engaged my brain, which was a relief after the typing experience. The Records department was staffed twenty-four hours a day, done in three shifts. I worked five days on, two days off, with the timing of my shifts varying. My sleep was all over the place. I took up doing jigsaws in my downtime, which I absolutely loved. It also suited my brain, which liked putting things together.

Shifts were intense. You'd stay in the one room in a guarded underground complex and be given food in there. I'd be tasked with things like working out the tonnage of a ship to see if it agreed with their workings, as a sort of cross-check. I had always been at the top of my class in math at school and loved solving problems, so this was right up my alley.

If someone wanted a file, their department would send a courier over. We had a secure system where a yellow light would come on and a buzzer would sound to tell me that a courier was on their way. When I had found the file and done any work I needed to with it, I would also press a buzzer and a light would come on at their end to let them know the courier was on the way. I remember on one occasion, the courier was three minutes late and still hadn't gotten to me—so I did what I was supposed to do and pressed the emergency button. It caused a major scare and the whole place was locked down. But it was the right thing to do. If the courier had been intercepted, it would have meant a security breach. The courier was soon found dead, but he had died of a heart attack rather than foul play.

During my time in Records I got to know Henry Hulme. He was married to Marion, and they had a daughter, Juliet, who was two by then. Little did either of us know back in 1940 that we would both later immigrate to New Zealand to make a new life on the other side of the world. I stayed there, though. Henry left after Juliet, in her teens by then, was convicted of the murder of her friend's mother in 1954. We stayed in touch over the years and I remember talking to him about it. The case rocked New Zealand at the time. When Juliet was released, she became British author Anne Perry— writer of historical detective fiction.

The year I spent working at the Admiralty in Scotland was a period when the war became an unavoidable part of daily life for the people of Britain. War was on their soil now, and it was a battle of survival. The Battle of Britain—fought, over English soil, between the RAF and the Luftwaffe for air superiority—started in July 1940. It was followed by large-scale night attacks on towns and cities—known as the Blitz—which continued through to May 1941. The Luftwaffe had gone from targeting coastal-shipping convoys and ports, to attempting to wipe out RAF Fighter Command in the air and on the ground, to eventually turning their attention to the terror-bombing of civilians and places of political significance.

From early September 1940, London was systematically bombed day and night, and other cities were targeted too. Very few areas were left untouched by air raids. The pictures of devastation we would see in the daily papers were heartbreaking: buildings reduced to rubble, houses half-standing with people's personal possessions exposed and furnishings waving in the breeze for all to see. A dinner table waiting for dinners. Fires burning, historical monuments destroyed, vast swathes of cities reduced to a crumbling mess—and always the homeless, devastated new refugees. Often they would be looking desperately through the debris—sometimes for precious possessions, sometimes for loved ones. Looking at the pictures, I wondered how on earth these places and the people in them would ever recover. By the time Hitler moved the Luftwaffe's focus toward Russia, in June 1941, over 43,500 civilians in Britain had been killed.

Even the royal family wasn't immune from the Blitz—the casualties at Buckingham Palace almost included King George VI and his wife, Queen Elizabeth. They had chosen to remain at Buckingham Palace in solidarity with those living through the Blitz, which endeared them to the everyday men and women coping with the chaos of the conflict. After the palace was bombed, the Queen was reported to have said: "I am glad we have been bombed. Now we can look the East End in the eye." It was a demonstration of the steely resilience of the British people. They were not about to give in to Hitler.

I visited London a few times during this period, through my growing friendship with Barbara Cox, a scientist working at the Admiralty. Accompanying her on visits to her family home in North Wembley, I became used to taking cover in underground air-raid shelters. I took all my holidays with Barbara and her family for many years, including after I had left the Admiralty. They became my wartime family and were really important to me. Barbara would be the only person I confided in when I was told I was going to France as an SOE agent. Like the good friend she was, she kept my secret, and her family only knew after the war.

One winter's day, Barbara's sister asked me to help her on her community nursing rounds. There was an old lady on her own who needed checking on. The old dear had gotten it into her head that she had to secure her front door in case any people displaced by the bombings broke in to steal things, and she had continued to add more and more to the barricade. For the first few days she was okay, but soon she had no food, no coal, and could not get herself out. She had managed to make herself a prisoner in her own home.

Looking up at the house, I saw a tiny window up high. It was a stiff climb and a tight squeeze, but I did it. I found the old lady huddled up in a bed in the darkness, absolutely freezing and not capable of helping herself at all. It took me quite some time to free the main door of debris and then work out how to undo her self-imposed security system so I could get her some help. This would not be the last time I'd be climbing walls and working out how to access places that I was not meant to be in.

* * *

IN MAY 1941, AN event happened that really brought the war home to me. I was asked to pull the file for HMS *Hood*. The ship had been attacked and had exploded in a spectacular fashion, sinking within minutes. All but three of the crew of 1,418 men had been killed, and the sinking was huge news.

I had made friends with quite a few of the sailors on HMS *Hood* before she sailed. Now they were all on the ocean floor. It was personal. I'd had enough of admin and I wanted out. I felt that there was more I could be doing for the war effort beyond managing naval records in Scotland.

I heard they were recruiting in Glasgow, so I snuck out on one of my weekends to see what the possibilities were. The recruitment form asked what I liked or didn't like doing. Was I interested in administrative work? No. Was I interested in outdoor work? Going abroad? "Yes," I answered, and then added the word "strongly" to both, to press the point home. Having spent the last year cooped up in a single room, I was ready for some fresh air and a change of scenery.

I also alerted the recruiters to my linguistic abilities, as well as reiterating that I did not want to be in admin. "No office work of any kind, but active work involving interpretation duties in order that my knowledge of languages may not be wasted." While my language skills weren't used in the first job I was posted to, they certainly must have been noted for use later.

I decided to volunteer at the RAF window—no khaki underwear for me—and then had to confess to Henry Hulme what I had done.

"I'm sad to see you go," he said. "Still, I can understand you've had enough of the underground life."

I joined the Women's Auxiliary Air Force, known as the WAAF, in November. Their purpose was to substitute, where possible, women for RAF personnel, to free the men up for other operational duties. Tens of thousands of women had volunteered to serve since the start of the war; conscription for women was only introduced in December 1941—a month after I had volunteered.

My posting was to a balloon unit near Edgbaston in Birmingham, where I served all through 1942 and into 1943. Barrage balloons were large balloons flown over cities and strategic locations to help with air defenses. When I say large, they really were—about fifty-six feet long with a twenty-three-foot diameter, tethered to the ground with huge steel cables. They were a common sight over cities, industrial areas, ports and harbors, where their role was to deter low-flying enemy aircraft, forcing them to fly higher where they would be at the mercy of RAF fighters and antiaircraft artillery fire. Balloons were hard to see on nighttime bombing raids or in fog, and made it more challenging for the enemy to attack ground targets. If low-flying aircraft did get under them, the traps on the steel cables would not be friendly either. If an enemy bomber snagged a cable, a mechanism would cause a section of cable with parachutes at either end to be explosively released. The combination of weight and drag would bring the aircraft down. It was these traps that I was involved with, and I enjoyed it. It appealed to my mathematical brain.

Despite the seriousness of war, there was always the opportunity for a bit of fun. An ack-ack (antiaircraft) battery unit, staffed by men, soon joined us and provided some nice social opportunities for us all. It was also not uncommon to see some of the girls trying to take a ride when the balloons were being inflated, with them having to let go when they got to a certain height. I recall another occasion when we were warned that a damaged RAF bomber was limping home to an airfield and we were to bring the balloons down. When they got through, there was a big collective cheer from us all before the balloons all went up again.

*　*　*

SOMETIMES I SOCIALIZED AT the WAAF Overseas Club, where there would be people who had come back from France. I always sought them out because I was keen to know what was happening on the ground there. One day the recent arrests in Paris were being discussed, and I heard Grandfather's name. The word was that he hadn't been able to keep his mouth shut about General Philippe Pétain, who had become head of the collaborationist regime of Vichy France in June 1940, so had been arrested. I was shocked, but not surprised—Grandfather was a man of principle. In World War I he had been an army general under Pétain, commander of the French Army at the time, and they knew each other. Grandfather would have been disgusted at him giving in to the Germans and would have said so openly. I hoped he was imprisoned just briefly, to give him a scare to shut him up. As it was next to impossible to stay in touch with them in wartime, in my mind I kept him and Josianne safe and well in Montparnasse, as I had left them. My contact offered to seek more information on him to get me an update.

On a subsequent visit to the Overseas Club, I received two shocking pieces of bad news. Firstly, Grandfather was dead. After his arrest he had not been seen again, and it was thought that he had been executed by the Germans. Alternatively, he might have died of a heart attack. He had already suffered two, and the stress of being arrested could easily have triggered another. There was no way of telling—but regardless, it did not undo the appalling fact that he had been imprisoned for speaking out against the Vichy regime in occupied France.

In that moment, the world stopped turning for me. And there was worse to come.

Josianne had committed suicide. Although this would not be confirmed until after the war, I presumed at the time that the intel was correct. Hers was quite a specific situation, so the story identified her easily. When she was asked by the Germans to reopen her school for the benefit of the wives of the German officers, who wanted to learn French, her refusal landed her in prison. Word was she was put in a cell that was extra-hot one minute and extra-cold the next, to put pressure on her. They gave her some water, but no food, for three days and waited for her to break. Finally she agreed to reopen the school, which gained Josianne her release.

My godmother had absolutely no intention of being forced to teach French to her German oppressors—and suicide was her chosen course of action. She was originally a nurse, so I presume she took an overdose of sleeping tablets. Josianne's final duty was to make sure her home could never be used for teaching again—and (probably at her suggestion) the French Resistance closed the school permanently with grenades soon after her death. The place she had created, with such love, to teach impressionable young women could now never be used to teach older women who supported Hitler's worldview.

Yet again, close family had been taken away from me in traumatic circumstances. I wanted to avenge their deaths—as a balloon operator in Birmingham, I had no way of exacting it. The wish for revenge is what drove me to get on the ground in France with SOE. Like Grandfather and his daughter, I had morals that I lived by, and would even die by, to secure a freedom I desperately wanted to protect.

FIVE

A CHANGE OF SERVICE

AS IT TRANSPIRED, THE ROUTE TO SOE WAS SOMEwhat circuitous. A few months into 1943, I was offered new work—as either a driver or a flight mechanic. I couldn't see myself driving officers around (a mistake, really, because I would also have learned motor mechanics and had a job after the war), so I took the flight mechanic role and was posted to St. Athan in South Wales. The training took seven or eight months and I passed all the exams. My next posting, in November 1943, had me going to London. I thought this strange because there was no airfield there, but I was told I had been requested to go to London for some interviews before taking up the specific posting. This I duly did.

A man in his late thirties, Albert Willis, met me off the train. He was accompanied by a woman in a First Aid Nursing Yeomanry (FANY) uniform, who grabbed my kit bag while Albert and I introduced ourselves.

"Who is she?" I asked.

"Our driver," he replied. Ah yes, I thought, the job I should have taken.

"Are you hungry?" he asked. I said I was absolutely famished.

We were driven right to the front door of the Lyons tea room in Piccadilly, a very nice part of town. The Lyons Corner Houses were a household name, and this was their popular flagship shop, bursting with diners. Even bombing did not stop the enjoyment of a nice meal at Lyons. If diners were interrupted mid-meal, as they often were, they could either take their food with them or were given a card to come back and finish their meal after they could leave the safety of the bomb shelters.

The food at Lyons was good, and we finished off with a cup of cocoa. Everything was cocoa back then—there was no coffee, no tea. Over lunch I learned a little more about Albert and what was in store for me.

"After lunch we are off to a place called Orchard Court. They are interested in talking to you about the languages you speak and whether there might be a job that you could be useful for."

At last, I thought, and let him know that this was something I was keen on.

"I am going to introduce you to a Major Jepson," Albert continued. "He's a very nice chap and he will go through a bit of your history. There are a few others to meet, too."

Albert explained that if the job was one I was interested in doing, he would be the officer overseeing my training. He had recently come back from France, but "at his age" was too old to go back. His job was now to stay in England and help people like me.

Orchard Court, at the southern end of Baker Street, housed residential apartments on a street that was otherwise shops and offices. After waiting for a short time in a hallway area upstairs, I was invited into a room where three Army officers were waiting. With three pips apiece, they were all captains, while I, as an aircraftwoman, only had a single-bladed propeller on my arm. I was very proud of that propeller, though, and I liked wearing blue.

For about ten minutes, I was questioned about my childhood in Africa, the languages I spoke, and my war service to date. I asked nothing myself—I didn't feel like this was a place to ask questions. And I could always ask Albert later.

From his accent, I could tell that one of the captains was from Mauritius. They roll their "r"s there, and so did my mother who was also from Mauritius. Because I speak Flemish, I don't roll my "r"s— mine are in my throat. This man was introduced to me as Claude de Baissac, who had recently come back from France. After the initial niceties he sauntered over to the table behind me, filled a mug with cocoa and brought it to me.

"Oh," I said, "thank you very much but I've just come from Lyons Corner House and I've had cocoa, but put it down here," and gestured to an appropriate spot beside me. I saw his mouth tighten.

He put the mug down slowly and with purpose, then turned and went off to a different part of the room. I had plainly offended him, and instantly realized what he must have been thinking. There's me, a little whippersnapper—no rank at all—giving him, a man of rank, an order. The colonial thing came in, too. I was white; he was not. He clearly felt that I was looking down on him, though I wasn't. I didn't mean to give him the wrong impression—that I was giving him an order. It was just that I *couldn't* drink a second cup of cocoa.

Next was a session with two Belgian women who wanted to know all about the languages I spoke, particularly French. I was tested first on my French, then one of the women tested me on Walloon—a

French-sounding language that isn't French, spoken on the Belgian border. The other woman tested me on my Flemish, which is the type of Dutch spoken in northern Belgium. And then they said— which I knew—that all my languages were accented with Flemish.

I then had an interview with Colonel Maurice Buckmaster, who was (not that I knew it at the time) the leader of the French (F) section of SOE. All the F Section women came through Orchard Court to be sized up, and by this time he had met quite a few in this building. Colonel Buckmaster talked to me about the importance of gathering French intelligence, particularly at this stage of the war. I warmed to him. He finished our brief conversation by introducing me to his personal assistant, Vera Atkins, a stylish-looking woman in her midthirties dressed in a nicely tailored civilian suit. She seemed to know quite a bit about me, and talked about my childhood in the Belgian Congo. Again this seemed somewhat strange to me, given the intelligence/translation position I thought was on offer. Unknown to me then, she was far more than just Buckmaster's assistant. Vera was responsible for all of the F Section women and took a personal interest in them, even after the war ended.

Finally, I was called into an interview with Major Jepson. Albert had told me that some checks had already been done on me and it was now up to Jepson to decide my suitability. Selwyn Jepson was indeed "the nice chap" that Albert had billed him as. Again unknown to me at the time, Jepson was the force behind recruiting women into SOE—often in the face of quite some opposition. In a postwar interview he plainly stated why he felt that women were much better for the work than men: "Women have a greater capacity for cool and lonely courage than men, who usually want a mate with them. Men don't work alone; their lives tend to be always in company with other men. Women are mostly on their own." He knew that women would do the job well, even getting Churchill on his side.

Major Jepson introduced himself as a recruiting officer. While our conversation covered much the same ground as the previous interviews, he also probed me about my feelings toward Germany. The recent deaths of Josianne and Grandfather were, naturally, at the forefront of my mind, and so I had no trouble talking about my hatred of the Nazi regime. Jepson was also interested in my nomadic childhood, where I had been very happy without set rules. He finished by saying that the job would require me to be in the FANYs.

"Might you like to think about it?" he asked.

Still quietly wondering what "the job" was, I told him I was happy to be considered for a new role. At no point had anyone said what it entailed. I concluded it was probably translating interviews with people coming in from France who had intelligence information.

* * *

SHORTLY AFTERWARD, ALBERT TOLD me that the interview process was over. I had passed, and would start the new role immediately. I would be staying in a hotel for the night, then Albert would pick me up to start training the next day at a location out of town. It would be my first and last night in a hotel. I would be sharing a room with another recruit and would also receive my FANY uniform there, because the new position required a new uniform.

The large Regent Palace Hotel was close to Piccadilly Circus in the heart of London. As we entered it, it was clear that he knew the place well because he greeted the doorman by name. Key in hand, I headed up to the designated room, reflecting on what an unusual day it had been so far and wondering how it would end. Perhaps the other recruit might know more than I did about what the new role was?

The door was opened by a pleasant-looking young woman with a welcoming expression. I instantly liked her.

"I'm Lilian," she offered as she held out her hand to shake mine. "Lilian Rolfe."

"I'm Pippa—Pippa Latour," I replied as she ushered me quickly into the room and shut the door.

We had obviously both been given the same brief—not to share any information with one another, particularly about our personal lives. That did not work. We sat on the beds and told each other a little about ourselves. I learned that she had a twin and had grown up in France, spent a little time in England, and until very recently had lived in Brazil. I gave her a condensed history of my travels before we quickly got to the elephant in the room—what it was we had signed up for.

"What do you think the job actually entails?" I asked her.

"It must be some sort of intelligence-gathering using our French, don't you think?" came her reply.

Agreeing, I added that given we were both in the WAAF, maybe we would be posted to airfields in England to talk to returnees. It was a relief to be able to talk to someone about this secretive position we had both found ourselves in. Lilian looked a little sheepish when she confessed that she had also shared information with her father. "I know I was not meant to talk to anyone, but I have mentioned it to my papa."

"What does he think?" I asked, wondering what an outsider would make of it all.

"He thinks it might be a safe job here in England and we won't be sent abroad. He seems very relieved."

After a while we went downstairs and enjoyed a high tea—it felt somewhat surreal to have two fancy meals at two fancy places in one day. Not long after we went back to our room, there was a knock on the door: it was Vera Atkins with our FANY uniforms. "Good evening, ladies," she said. "I am pleased you have met. Now let's get you suited up as is now appropriate to your new role."

She did not give much away about what would happen next, simply saying that we would be picked up separately by our conducting officers in the morning to commence training. Vera cut a fine figure in her lovely suit, and plainly took pride in the way she looked. After we had changed, she looked us up and down in our new FANY uniforms, made sure that they fitted nicely, then stepped back and said, quietly, "Welcome to the FANYs, ladies." She took our WAAF uniforms away with her, although I insisted on keeping my blue underwear—no khaki for me. Although eventually I was officially let go from the WAAF, I was always a WAAF at heart and would always wear my blue underwear.

Next morning, Lilian was picked up first. As I farewelled her at the door, I wondered when we would next see each other on this strange journey we both now found ourselves on. Albert turned up for me with the same FANY driver. It took us a lot longer to get out of London than it should have because there were two bombing raids where we had to stop the car and make a mad dash to the underground. We wondered who was getting it this time. You heard the *boom, boom* of it, and you just hoped that it wouldn't come closer.

As we drove, Albert told me I would be going to a few different training venues around the country in the next few months.

We eventually pulled up at a beautiful country estate where I would be staying for a time. Winterfold House, near Cranleigh in Surrey, was the site of the Student Assessment Board where prospective agents had their initial training over a period of about four weeks—which was all of November for me. It was the initial sift-and-sort process, where those deemed unsuitable were weeded out.

I found out later that the in-joke was that SOE stood for "Stately 'omes of England," reflecting the gracious country manors the organization had requisitioned for training. After a nice dinner in the company of a few others, I was shown to a stately room complete with a four-poster bed and fell asleep while wondering what lay ahead.

The regular food and sleep I had here in the coming days were not to be the norm in other places. Between December 1943 and March 1944 I would go to various stately homes to learn all manner of things with small groups of people. There were exhausting commando courses, rope-climbing, and running with a full pack. As well as getting fit, we were trained in weaponry. Of course I enjoyed shooting and, having been introduced to it at a young age, was quite capable there. Depending on where they deemed you useful—radio operator, courier, saboteur—and the skills you would therefore need to master, SOE agents learned variously about hand grenades, numerous explosives, and a large variety of knives and daggers—and how to use all of them to either injure or kill. Some of the explosives were quite covert and disguised in things like cigarettes and cow dung. There were knives and even guns that could be concealed up your sleeve, and—for the ladies—daggers disguised as hat pins. The caltrop, an age-old device, was used to burst the tires of vehicles or injure foot soldiers, and we also needed to be experts at pulling apart a Sten submachine gun and putting it back together, even in the dark. Silent killing was also a skill to master.

We also did training in the use of the Eureka beacon, which was used to direct aircraft to a specific point on the ground to deliver supplies or to pick up agents, and the S-Phone, which was a two-way UHF radio used to communicate with aircraft.

And then there was the people side of things—organizing reception committees to collect the people and items being dropped into France, connecting with the Resistance and the Maquis (who were elements of the Resistance located in more isolated areas), plus a crash course in the various political factions on the ground and the organization of the German military. Classes on secrecy included devices like bolts that unbolted so you could hide messages inside, lessons on communicating stealthily in full sight of others, how to look for the unusual as a sign; all sorts of things. How to fit in like a local was another focus—don't take your beret off inside, don't look right when you cross a road, don't put the milk in before the tea.

It did not take me too long to realize that the job I was training for was *not* translating intelligence interviews on English soil. Instead, I was in an intensive training scheme for secret agents being prepared to be dropped behind enemy lines in France.

★ ★ ★

I THINK THE TRUTH actually hit at the second stately home, in northwest Scotland. This was STS 22—Rhubana Lodge in Morar, near Mallaig. My paramilitary training took place there. It was tough going. I couldn't understand whether they were trying to kill us or what in training, but our group of four would be dropped off somewhere to make our own way back. We didn't know where we were, but had to avoid villages on our way back to our starting point at the house. Getting back was hard work, particularly in midwinter, and you needed to have your wits about you—and when you got back, there was no dinner. One time, we were told the cook was sick or some such thing. I had spied some jigsaws in the living area, and since I've always loved them, I put my mind to completing one that evening rather than get too fussed about the lack of food (like the three men I was with were doing).

The next morning we were all woken up very early, and of course the cook was still sick—so there was no breakfast before our hour-long route march. Even that wasn't simple. They would make us run, walk, do certain steps, etc., at different times—all meant to test us. When we got back, still no breakfast. By now we hadn't eaten for a good twenty-four hours. They said that the cook had gone and someone else was coming to replace him that afternoon. We all went back to bed again, then were woken up two hours later, at about nine o'clock in the morning, for our Morse practice. And still nothing to eat. We finally got fed at about 2 P.M.

We never had a good night's sleep at that place. We would often be woken up about three o'clock in the morning and dropped off somewhere remote to find our way home. Food was intermittent. Things were totally random, and you came to expect the unexpected.

They tried to break you in other ways, too. There was this one Scotsman who spoke with a French accent who was *so* picky. A real bastard. In his book, nothing was ever right. Whatever you did, he would always find fault with it and make you do the whole thing over again. One time it was the wrong walking/running order, and that we had gone too close to a village when finding our way back to base. So, we had to do the whole thing over again, which took about three hours. Another time it would be something else.

One day at shooting practice I got so enraged with him—internally, of course. We were in this kind of barn where multiple images on targets would pop up and down. Some were "good," like a woman pushing a pram, while others were "bad," and we had to make quick judgments and shoot accurately at the "bad" ones. Photos of our instructors were on some of the "good" targets. I was so irate with this Scotsman that when his target image popped up, I shot it in the crotch. And that was when he, and my fellow shooters, realized that I could shoot—and shoot well. They were shocked because I had never tried to do better than the men, a carryover from my childhood.

I later found out that this instructor's attitude had purposely been like that—to prepare us for interrogation. I met him after the war, and he was actually very nice. "Pippa," he said, "being an instructor was awful. I knew how much you all hated me."

Another man, called Green, just appeared one day, telling us he had served time for burglary and it was his job to pass on what he knew. We started with ropes, and trained on scaffolding that mimicked buildings; we had to go from one to another without touching the ground. While I had never used ropes, the training was reminiscent of playing with the monkeys in my childhood when I was bored and had nobody to play with. As the monkeys went from tree to tree I would chase them, swinging from one branch to get to another if needed. It was fun, and of course as a kid I was fearless. Green taught us how to throw an anchor from one roof to another, climb across on the rope, and then loosen the anchor to take with us. While the others were fearful of the heights, this was literally child's play for me. With a look of surprise, Green told me, "You're good at the ropes, Pippa."

The next task was to get into a multistory house stealthily through a top window. Green taught us how to go up and down a drainpipe using our knees, and how to crawl over a roof without casting a silhouette—on your stomach, not on your knees. You were crawling like a crab. Once up there, we learned how to get in and out of the window. As I successfully squeezed inside, I was reminded of my time with Barbara Cox's sister in London—getting into the old lady's home to rescue her. Green told me I was a "natural" and to come to him for a job after the war! I did correspond with him for five or six years postwar. I called him the "gentle cat burglar" because he was a Robin Hood type of character. He told me one story about how he had taken something from a house that he later heard was very dear to the owner because it had belonged to her late husband—so he secretly returned it. I thought at the time of our training that he was a "good sort" of burglar.

★ ★ ★

OUR TRAINING ALSO COVERED interrogation. There were people who had already been to France who talked about it, so we had some real-world experience to call on. We were drilled in how to lie to give yourself the best chance of things not becoming worse. For example, if you were asked where you were it was better not to say somewhere specific like a cinema, because then you'd be asked what was on, what time it was, what you saw in the film. It was better to be general, like saying you were at the market.

As my conducting officer, Albert was involved in my training. He talked to me about trying to avoid being interrogated in the first place, reiterating to me the danger I would be in once I was in France. Firstly, there were a lot of double agents and collaborators over there, and it would be hard to know who to trust. Albert was speaking from personal experience—the reason he was back in England was because he had been betrayed in France and he'd had to get out quickly. Secondly, I should not rely on the Geneva Convention to keep me safe if I was captured. As we were FANYs and thus allowed to carry arms, in theory we should be protected under the convention just as the men were.

The reality was that—according to Hitler and his Commando Order—the Geneva Convention did not apply to Special Forces personnel, who would be treated as spies. If caught, we would likely be tortured before being executed without trial.

"Six weeks," Albert told us. He meant that was the current life expectancy for a radio operator, which was to be my role. "The trick is not to be caught," he said, before going on to tell us about the use of the "L" pill—the cyanide suicide tablet—that we would be issued with if that was our wish.

Alfred also explained that the top-secret nature of the job required me to sign a document issued by the Special Training Schools (STS) that I was attending. It noted that I was never to disclose to anyone any information that I had acquired in my time there or in the future, and if I did so I would have disciplinary measures taken against me under the Official Secrets Act 1911, the Treachery Act

1940, and Defense Regulations. I took that oath seriously, never speaking about this part of my life until my old age.

* * *

I HAD BEEN CHOSEN to be a radio operator early in my training. Learning Morse code was a staple part of our training; a life-and-death one. Early on we were trained in the basics, and if you were found to be good at it you then lived and breathed Morse. My childhood love of Morse had now turned into a job. The birds seemed to be chirping in Morse, and I was probably dreaming in Morse! We first concentrated on accuracy and then getting our speed up. At one of the last country estates, I was selected to join a small group of radio operators who were ahead of things, and we were trained separately. But before I got there, we all had to learn how to parachute-jump.

It was mid-January 1944 and I had moved to Dunham House, a beautiful brick manor house near RAF Ringway, which is now Manchester Airport. Dunham House was just a number to me, though—all the training places were, because none of us were told their names or locations in case we were interrogated and gave the information away. Dunham House was STS 51.

I did not enjoy my time at Ringway—I found jumping scary. We had three static-line jumps to complete, where a fixed line deploys the parachute rather than the parachutist. One jump was from a cage slung underneath a huge balloon and the other two were from bomber aircraft, one during the day and one at night. We would jump as a "stick," which means a group of paratroopers, usually six of us at a time. I always went out first but came down last because I was so light.

I had a perfect jump from the balloon, which was a good start, but in the first (daylight) parachute jump from the aircraft I couldn't control my parachute and landed on top of another parachutist. Darkness made things even more intimidating, but I completed the jump. When I was issued with a second-grade pass for the course, I asked if I could do it again—not because I liked it but because I wanted a first-grade pass. Annoyingly they turned me down, saying that there was no time for another attempt and I should be good enough to parachute into occupied France, if that was what was required of me. I secretly hoped I would be landing on the ground in a Lysander airplane, like some other Allied spies, instead.

The next stop was STS 52 (Thame Park, in Oxfordshire), where the radio operator work came into sharp focus. Although they wanted us to be the best we could be with our Morse and encoding, we were told that some mistakes were natural—and expected. We would be working in haste to ensure we were not caught, and that often meant that a few letters would not be quite right. If a message came through completely perfect, it was a red flag that it was likely fake; in part because the sender would have had time to write the message out with no mistakes. We needed speed because by 1944 the direction-finding equipment had improved significantly and the Germans could triangulate to find you in twenty to thirty minutes. This meant we needed to keep our messages down in length, ideally to about a hundred letters, so that we could send, shut down, and leave as quickly as possible.

The advanced group I was in comprised me and three men who were also doing well with Morse. One was a Dutchman, whom I was quite friendly with, and the other two were Belgians. They were twice my age, in their forties, and one of the Belgians had already been to France. We were told that our group had been selected to travel while we were over there—most of the other radio operators would be static with one set, but we would be on the move and accessing multiple sets.

At one point the instructors took me off on my own to train for a period, because my speed was faster than the men's and they wanted to check my work. I was trialing a new Morse transmitting key and really liked it. Nobody else seemed interested in it. It was much smaller and operated using a side key, which was a bit hard to get used to, but of course I loved solving problems. My wrist didn't need to move, just my fingers. Naughtily I purloined the key at the end of the training rather than handing it in. Nobody knew I had kept the key, and as far as I know I'm the only one who used one of those during the war.

Our tuition on the radio set was thorough. We were taught about the parts of it and how it worked, about the pieces that often needed replacing, like valves, and about the all-important portable quartz crystals we would carry to tune us into the correct frequency to contact home base. These crystals also needed replacing at times, and we were trained in the basics of diagnosis and repair. There would be regular drops of parts with which to repair sets, and it was the courier's job to get them to and from the places they were needed.

Even though we would be given a "sked"—a scheduled time of day to connect—a FANY would always be on hand to receive our messages, twenty-four hours a day. We had a "true" and a "false" code to give as we connected, so that home base would know if we were in trouble. Coding was a complicated discipline that was a closely held secret. I was asked to choose a poem that I would have no trouble remembering; home base would have a copy of it, too, attached to my name. I chose a Flemish poem about *regendropje* (raindrops) that I had learned off by heart as a little girl at school in the Belgian Congo. I would send four letters from my poem to show that I was the person sending it. They had to be consecutive, but could be backward or forward. Then home base would know it was actually me. The codes I would use to encrypt my messages were printed on a small piece of silk, which I needed to hide on my person. This system was unbreakable if both sender and receiver kept to the rules. Each code could only be used once and would have to be destroyed.

Here, my love of math, Morse, and jigsaws were all rolled into one enjoyable problem-solving job. After much practice, encoding, sending, and decoding became second nature to me. However, it was one thing to do this cosseted away in a training facility in England, and another to do it under pressure in France. I was determined to become as skilled as possible.

Toward the end of our training, radio operators were dropped off in pairs for practice missions. We would be dropped in all weathers (snow included), in all sorts of places, to practice our craft. I got to see Lilian Rolfe again, briefly, because she too had become a radio operator. It was lovely to see her smiling face when we paired up together one time. Before we parted ways, Lilian and I agreed on a postwar plan to meet up in Trafalgar Square in London at a certain date and time. It was a random, romantic notion really, but we stashed the thought away as a nice possibility.

The next time, we were not together. They kept us guessing as to who was around on these country estates. I met another female radio operator I also warmed to. Denise Bloch was a couple of years younger than Lilian, so only five years older than me. I liked spending time with Denise in our training—we women in our twenties felt an instant affinity with each other.

The last stop for me was STS 35—Beaulieu, another mansion on a beautiful big estate, this time in the New Forest, a national park in southern England. Known as the SOE Finishing School, it was where I was to polish my skills and wait for the call. I had expected to spend quite some time here, but that was not to be. Soon, Albert told me that the "Baker Street irregulars" (the nickname for SOE) had a pressing job for me in France. We were to head back to London to prepare.

SIX

FAREWELL, ENGLAND

BACK AT ORCHARD COURT ON BAKER STREET, THINGS felt different. The last time I had been here, I was being interviewed for a job where I wasn't even sure what was involved. Now I knew full well what I was up for. Well, not completely—I felt they never really told you *everything*.

Before going into a meeting with Maurice Buckmaster and Vera Atkins, Albert told me that three people who had been stationed in the area I would be going were no longer at their posts, and a replacement radio operator was needed to travel the Normandy coast. Did that mean these people had been killed? Or were they captured and now prisoners of war? I presumed the latter, but did not ask for details.

Buckmaster and Vera began by thanking me for taking on the task. These were both people I had respected from the instant we met. It suddenly felt like a long time since I had first seen them, here at the start of my SOE journey, yet it was only a few months ago. I had learned a lot in the interim. We moved straight to the business of getting me on my way, with Albert beginning the briefing.

"Dr. Paul Janvier is a doctor based in Bais. He runs the local Navarre Resistance network there and will provide you access to a safe house straightaway. There is also a vet and a grocer you can trust—you will know these men simply by numbers. It is Paul who will be your first and primary contact on the ground there, and he will advise you further. Use his name on arrival."

Vera went through the key information I needed to be aware of. My code names—Lampooner in England and Plus Fours in France—were never to be mixed up. Baker Street—SOE's headquarters, a few blocks away along the road—would give me a different identifying field name that I would not know. My alias story came with a false identity card for "Paulette," along with a ration card and a Certificate of Residence to show where I lived. All of these items needed to be carried on me at all times, because I would be asked to present them whenever I was stopped by the Germans.

Vera paused, then continued: "It is unusual, but you will be dropped on your own."

In our parachute training we had always gone in groups—two at a minimum. Jumping on your own was not usual. I thought Vera looked a little concerned about that.

Buckmaster then told me I would be working with the newly (re)formed Scientist network in Normandy as a radio operator. There would be a courier for me; he thought I would have the choice of a couple. My role was to be a roaming one—on the road gathering intelligence and sending that (and any information from others) to home base, as well as receiving any messages from England. Normandy was now a huge focus for both the Germans and the Allies, and it would not be safe for me to stay in any one place for very long.

This was the second time that a network had been called Scientist. The previous one had imploded in Bordeaux in 1943. Given that there was much experience to draw on from the people who were involved then, and the fact that they were prepared to go to France again, there was great hope that this network would make good progress at this crucial time. The war was moving quickly; there was talk that the Allies would be on the ground on the Continent in the coming weeks. They needed to get me across quickly to get information on what was happening along the Normandy coastline. Unless I went within the next few days, with a full moon to provide sufficient light for night flying, it would be another month—the end of May—and potentially too late.

Buckmaster finished his briefing by handing me a beautiful gold pen. "Keep this safe, and bring it back with you." He smiled. "But if you need to make it into ready cash over there, it is good currency for you."

There was much to organize before I left—photos, false identity cards, and plans for both my departure and my arrival—and I would stay at Orchard Court for the night while everything was put in place. I was to report back in a couple of hours, but until then I was free to enjoy London. Just as I turned to walk out of the door, I heard Vera pipe up again.

"One last thing before you go, Pippa. If you change your mind about taking this on, you can do so at any time. Right up until you jump."

I wondered if that had ever happened, but she continued before I could ask.

"I must let you know we have had some refuse the mission, even over the target, so you would not be the first."

"What happened to them?" I asked, wondering whether that was confidential information or not.

"They were not sent back to their original unit," said Vera, "but rather offered an administrative job somewhere else." She stressed that this was not a downward move. "There is an opportunity there to work toward an officer commission, too."

I suspect I looked somewhat unconvinced that there would not be any repercussions from the system or any personal ill-feeling, because Vera was quick to reassure me.

"These are people we don't want to lose, and we are very grateful they speak up and make that decision before they get onto the ground there in France, where it is rather hard work. It is better for everyone if they do. It would not be cowardly to speak up and change your mind—in fact, it is brave to do so."

I could see Vera watching me closely as she spoke. It was, obviously, not what they would want with any person they had trained for months, but—while not encouraging the option—she needed to give me permission to take it.

"Don't worry, I won't change my mind," I said as I left the room.

★ ★ ★

THESE DAYS, THE BACK entrance of Orchard Court, off Seymour Mews, has been restored, with a majestic-looking wrought-iron gateway, which makes it look rather smart compared with the neighboring buildings. But back then the gate had been removed to aid the war effort. Wrought-iron railings and other metal objects were often collected in salvage drives around London, to be repurposed for armament, ammunition, and other military equipment. SOE headquarters at 64 Baker Street was another innocuous-looking building. As I walked past, I glanced up at it with new eyes, now knowing how much was going on inside it.

Being in London was a treat after the past few months of training, and I enjoyed drinking the place in before I had to leave "Mother England" for an unknown period. I decided I would get my hair shampooed properly. I was blessed with curly hair, and with a fresh wash it set beautifully. On the walk back I saw a pair of red shoes, and bought them. I don't know what I was thinking; perhaps that I could leave them in England and have them to come back to. I was feeling pretty good about myself.

Then I got back to Orchard Court. The FANY staff there took one look at me and told me that where I was going there was no shampoo. I simply could not arrive there with freshly washed hair smelling of shampoo—my cover would be blown and I'd be nabbed straightaway. Besides, how you washed your hair over there was also an open question; it might even not be washed at all for quite some time. I understood—but it smelled and felt so good. My hair was washed again over a basin, using Sunlight dish soap. *That* smell was acceptable, it seemed.

Of course, the shoes would not be going to France with me either. And there was something else I could not take—my monkey-foot charm given to me by Nyama. It had kept me safe, just as he had said it would, all the way from the Belgian Congo, to Kenya, to Paris, and now England, ever since I was twelve years old. Almost half my life. I quietly hoped it would continue to work its magic from afar.

By now, a "personal message" had been sent via the BBC's daily Radio Londres broadcast, to advise of my impending arrival. The program, which began airing in 1940, was entirely in French and was operated by Free French who had escaped from occupied France. Listened to across the Channel, it was used to send coded messages to the French Resistance, appeal for uprisings, provide hope, and counterbalance the propaganda sent out by the authorities in the occupied territory over German-controlled Radio Paris.

There's something interesting to know about the music the BBC used to open their Radio Londres bulletins with—the opening bars of Beethoven's Fifth Symphony, which goes "Di-di-di-dah." You will know it if you look it up. Morse code for the letter V is three short pulses and one long pulse (dit, dit, dit, dah . . .), so this opening translated to a musical Morse version of "V"—which by then meant "V for Victory." The V symbol—made famous by Winston Churchill holding his index and middle fingers up in a "V" shape—and its audio companion became part of everyday life in wartime. It was the rhythm of a knock on a door; the way teachers clapped to get attention from their class; it was even heard in church bells.

Radio Londres typically began its transmissions with: "Ici Londres! Les Français parlent aux Français." ("This is London! The French speaking to the French.") And then: "Before we begin, please listen to some personal messages," and a string of these would follow. Sometimes they meant something to someone, a prearranged code; sometimes they were simply nonsensical. For example, "Le chat a neuf vies" (The cat has nine lives) meant an agent drop, while "Je n'aime pas les crêpes Suzette" (I don't like crêpes Suzette) had no meaning. The multiplicity of phrases was intended to give the enemy the impression that something was being prepared when it might not have been. For those not in the know, the task of sifting out the legitimate from the ridiculous was impossible. The "genuine" phrases would alert certain reception groups that, say, an agent would be dropped into their area in the coming days. After the initial message had been sent, it was followed up with another one on the day the agent was to be dropped in—which in my case was the next day. I had one last full day in England.

After some more preparation the following morning, Vera took me out for lunch. I ordered fish and chips—a very English thing to eat. On the walk back, I looked at all the trees springing into life in Portman Square, directly opposite Orchard Court, and realized that it was the first day of May. Summer was not far away. The London weather, however, had not gotten the message, and my last day in England turned into a wet and windy, gray old day.

☆ ☆ ☆

ORCHARD COURT FELT LIKE an oasis—gracious, lovely, warm surroundings exuding a touch of luxury. I knew life was about to be anything but luxurious. A car would be here to pick up Vera and me later in the afternoon for the drive to the air base, a journey north of about two hours. I tried to rest, but my mind was busy.

As we left London, the weather became noticeably worse. I wondered for a moment that if it was like this on the ground, what would it be like in the air? Vera caught a faraway look in my eye as I was gazing at the bleak weather outside.

"Might be wise to have a sleep, while you can," she suggested.

I nodded my head in agreement. She asked me to close the curtains on the windows in the back compartment and said I should lie down. Presumably this was why she had offered to ride in the front of the staff car with the driver.

Ordinarily, getting to sleep in a moving car might have been hard, but the previous few days had been a whirlwind and I was tired. I am not sure how long I slept, but I woke to feel the car slowing down and a gentle hand on my shoulder from Vera, rousing me.

"We are here," she said.

Although I did not know its name at the time, "here" was RAF Tempsford, otherwise known as Gibraltar Farm and one of the most secret air bases in England. It is said that even the local farming community never really knew what was going on in their sleepy hollow. They knew that at the end of the road with the sign saying "This road is closed to the public" there was an RAF base, and on moonlit nights they would hear aircraft take off and land, but that was all. The purpose of the base's activity was unknown to them. It was from there in a marshy (and often foggy) landscape that SOE agents would leave England and return home. As well as their precious human cargo, the aircraft flying from RAF Tempsford delivered arms, ammunition, radio sets, food, and other supplies to the Resistance fighters in Europe.

I went to draw back the curtains on the car window to see where we were, but saw Vera shake her head at me. It was still daylight outside, and it seemed that I was secret cargo until we were safely inside the confines of the base itself.

Within a few minutes we were through the gate and I was allowed to open the curtains. The fish and chips I'd so happily eaten earlier were now not so happily sitting in my stomach. Perhaps it was sleeping in the car that made me feel sick. Perhaps it was nerves. Whatever it was, I was feeling unwell and I had to let Vera know: "I'm sorry, but I really feel like I want to be sick."

"Some fresh air will help," she said, "and we are almost where we need to be." I concentrated on what was out the window, to focus my mind away from my churning stomach.

In the distance I could see Army huts—aircraft hangars—with taxiways leading off them toward runways. This was no quiet, retiring farm down the end of a country lane—it was a busy operational base always ready to spring into life. I discovered later that RAF Tempsford had about a thousand personnel based there to support two Special Duties Squadrons. Between 1942 and 1945, Halifaxes and Stirlings (both heavy bombers), Hudsons and Lysanders flew in and out of the base with their cargoes to aid the secretive war effort in Europe. Hudsons and Lysanders were used to transport agents to and from France—effectively a taxi service. Hudsons could carry about ten passengers but needed twice the length of field in which to land. Lysanders, however, could land in under seven hundred feet but could only hold two agents. Instead of heading toward the aircraft hangars, we drove toward a forested area in the distance with a few farm buildings around it, including what seemed to be a farmhouse. I wondered if that was our destination, but we stopped instead at an old wooden barn that looked as if it had been there for many a year. On one side of it there was an opening wide enough for a vehicle to enter, which we duly did. Although the outside was wooden, as we drove slowly in I could see that the inside was all brick. It looked to be a preflight preparation area: a handful of people in different brick bays were checking equipment and looking at paperwork. I deduced that this was where I would be equipped. "Just the one, ma'am?" came the question from the man Vera had turned to as soon as she got out of the car.

"Yes, that is correct. Unusual, I know, but just the one."

Clearly they were both aware that normally more than one agent would be dropped at a time—they often went in groups of two or three. Not only was it highly unusual that I was going on my own, but once I got there I knew I would also be traveling on my own, too—equally unusual. As I listened to this brief interchange, I thought to myself that I might as well get used to being solitary because that would be my existence for the foreseeable future.

As I exited the vehicle myself I saw the man quickly and efficiently inspect me up and down, without disguising what he was doing. I wondered if he was sizing me up to see, in his measure at least, whether I would cope on my own. As I was now feeling better, I hoped I didn't look too insipid. I remembered the conversation two days earlier about it never being too late to change your mind, right up until you jumped out of the aircraft, and briefly wondered how many had done that here in this barn. The man's examining look stiffened my resolve. I quelled any feelings of anxiety, which were there if I chose to listen. I silenced those thoughts bubbling quietly away. I was ready for this.

"I'll just get an update on the weather," Vera said, signaling me to take a seat at one end of the barn. Within a couple of minutes there was an answer: the inclement weather that had stayed with us on the trip north from London would still be around for at least a couple more hours. This weather system extended to northern France and the designated drop zone was likely wet and windy. Wet was not too much of an issue, but wind certainly was. Parachuting into a specific area in the dark to meet the waiting reception committee was challenging enough for everyone involved without the wind blowing the parachutist off course. And landing in wind also brought the potential for being dragged into trees. Vera suggested that I use the waiting time to continue to catch up on sleep, and showed me a camp stretcher at the end of the barn.

"Thank you," I said, "I will do just that. I think it will help with how I am feeling, too"—hoping very much that it would.

* * *

THE SLEEP DID DO me a world of good. When I again felt Vera's hand on my shoulder to wake me up, I came to in a much-improved state, which was quite a relief. "It's time to get ready," she said.

As I walked to the other end of the barn, past the open door, I could see it was now well dark outside and the weather seemed to have eased. I looked at my watch and saw that it was just after 10:30 P.M. The countdown to my departure was on.

At the first brick bay, a man handed me a complete set of French clothing to get changed into behind a curtain. Everything had French labels, even the underwear. The mustard-colored skirt was plain in the front but pleated at the back, a bit like a Scotsman's kilt. The matching jacket, in the same color, had a blouse underneath of light green. I pulled back the curtain and handed the clothing I had taken off to the man waiting close by.

"Very good. They fit, then?" I nodded my head—they seemed to be a good enough fit.

"You'll be given a hat, gloves, and handbag in France. Watch, please." Of course, my English watch would have to stay in England. He then proceeded to pick up a pair of sensible-looking shoes from the bench beside my discarded English clothing. "These will go in your pockets when you are ready to go, but"—beckoning to

Vera—"first let's make sure there are no signs of Mother England anywhere on your person."

This seemed a strange statement, given that he had supplied the clothing, but apparently it was standard operating procedure to go through all the pockets to ensure there were no English bus cards, railway tickets, money, handkerchiefs, or the like. These would of course be an obvious giveaway if I was ever to be searched by the Gestapo. Vera did this task in silence, double-checking my pockets and the labels on all my clothing.

"And you have your codes we gave you in London?" she asked.

"Of course," I said, producing the piece of silk that would be my coding companion. She gave me a small nod to indicate that all was fine, and motioned to me to take a few steps forward to the next bay.

Here my paperwork was checked. My ration card, identity card, and Certificate of Residence had been given to me at Orchard Court, but we all knew it was a rush job given the haste with which it had been decided to send me. Vera went over all of them with me once again. "Never go anywhere without these. You will always be asked for them by the Germans."

Although I had seen my identity card before, in the rush of getting away I had not really paid any attention to it. Now I looked more closely. Most people who had identity cards made for them were thirty or forty years old, and I realized that the powers that be had presumed I would pass for a twenty-nine-year-old even though I had only very recently turned twenty-three. They had never even seen me to know whether I looked young or old for my age, but had simply deemed twenty-nine as appropriate.

"Who are you?" asked Vera.

"To you I am Lampooner, to the Resistance I am Plus Fours. To everyone else I am Paulette Jeannine Latour, born in Paris in the six-teenth arrondissement on the eighth of April 1915." I had no issue re-membering the month and day, as it was my actual birthday, though I'd been born in 1921. "I have just turned twenty-nine and been living in the Guillotière district in Lyon—on the left bank of the Rhône—for the past couple of years. My address there was 14 rue Jaboulay and I was working as a secretary until recently, when I moved north."

"Excellent," came her swift reply. "The rest of the story about the intricacies of why you are there you can sort out with the people on the ground in France, who will help you assimilate. I will leave you to get flight-ready now, and then we'll be off to the aircraft. It's not the usual transfer crew tonight, it seems, but they will tell us more soon."

The man who had given me my French clothing now brought over some more recognizable military clothing. The SOE striptease—that was the name the parachute jumpsuit was known by. It had two zippers on the front running parallel up the entire length of the overalls from the ankles to either side of the neck, enabling the wearer to discard them quickly with one pull of a leather tab. De-signed for onetime use, they were made of a heavy-duty windproof camouflage-pattern fabric with various internal and external pock-ets to house everything from a pistol, shovel, and knife to documents and maps. There was also a large pouch fitted to the rear in case an agent was taking a small parcel, suitcase, or attaché case with them.

Once I had zipped the jumpsuit up over my ladylike French suit, the man handed me the items destined for my pockets. Some items were innocuous, like my French shoes. Others were more in keeping with the new life I was about to embark on: flashlight, compass, sti-letto knife, revolver, Sten gun with ammunition. After he had ticked off most of the standard-issue items on his list, he turned to face me.

"I think we are almost there, but I do need to check something with you."

I met his earnest look.

"I understand you don't want the suicide tablet?"

"That is correct," I answered. I had thought about this for some time, having known it was a standard offering to people at high risk of capture, like me. The "L" tablet contained a fatal dose of cyanide, and if you bit down on it with force it would kill you within fifteen seconds. I had decided it was something I would never need, and therefore wouldn't bother with. It would just be another thing to worry about and I didn't need to have anything extra on my mind. I needed to concentrate on surviving, doing my job, and staying invisible and out of trouble.

"As you wish," he continued. "Here is the Benzedrine, though." The amphetamine was standard issue for operatives—taken to keep you awake when necessary—and I saw no harm in having it available to me.

He turned his attention to the map rolled out on the bench in front of him. "As you've been advised in London, you'll be dropped in the Mayenne in the Pays de la Loire region, western France. The crew have the coordinates. When you land, you will be met by the reception crew who will deal with your parachute and swiftly move you to appropriate cover."

The last thing I put on were some military-issue lace-up boots. They felt very heavy, but that was soon explained: "You are light, and to get you down quickly in a low-level drop and not be buffeted too far off course by any wind, we needed to weight your boots."

This time, Vera and I sat side by side in the back of the staff car for the last trip together to the waiting aircraft. There was one final parting surprise.

"Just to let you know, ladies, we were unable to secure an RAF aircraft this evening. OSS have helped us out at Harrington, and we have our American friends on the tarmac waiting for you."

The RAF aircraft that was supposed to drop me had been shot down over Holland. RAF Harrington, about an hour's drive away, was an airfield recently built by the US Army for heavy bomber use, and a couple of United States Army Air Forces (USAAF) Bombardment Squadrons were newly ensconced there in late March 1944. The mission of the Carpetbaggers, as they were known, was to fly Special Operations missions delivering supplies to Resistance groups in enemy-occupied countries, working with the OSS (the Office for Strategic Services), the intelligence agency of the United States during World War II.

"Your transfer to France tonight will be with the Crance crew of the 406th Bombardment Squadron in a B-24 Liberator. This is a first for them." And another first for me—as well as being the first woman to be dropped solo by the Americans, I would be the first SOE agent dropped by the Crance crew.

The door closed, the driver started the engine, and we slowly inched out of the barn.

"I'm glad you're feeling better, and you've had some sleep." Vera smiled.

"Well," I replied, "those fish and chips were the cheapest thing I could order, and I thought I was doing the right thing. Maybe I should have ordered something more expensive for our last lunch together—maybe that wouldn't have made me feel sick."

I added, wryly, "In France, at least I'll change my diet."

Vera's smile turned into a little laugh at my attempt at light humor; we both knew I would not be eating beautiful French food. I was to be always on the road, managing myself with only a courier for company and foraging for whatever we could find. If I was light now, I was going to weigh even less on my return.

"You have Buckmaster's pen, yes?"

I nodded. The gold pen, a standard personal parting gift from Buckmaster to his SOE agents, was indeed in one of my pockets, and I knew, as instructed by him, that I should give it to a safe person in France to keep for me in case I needed to sell it.

"I have something else for you," she continued. "This one is only for the women and comes from me to you."

She handed me a small gold compact. I opened it to see a delicate powder puff inside and caught my face in the little mirror. "Like the pen, if you get in trouble it is good currency, so find a safe home for it over there. And if you have no use for it there, bring it home with you."

To me, the idea of sitting in front of a mirror to powder my face seemed a lifetime away. This beautiful, feminine item was tied to a prewar existence that I quietly hoped would translate to a postwar one. I would always remember getting this precious wartime memory from Vera. She was a class act and I hugely respected her. Right at that moment, she felt like a true friend, someone who had my back.

She must have caught a look of vulnerability on my face. "You know you can change your mind, don't you? Even now. Even when you are halfway across the English Channel. Any time before you jump."

"Yes, I know," I quickly reassured her, "and I won't."

"Well, there is no shame in it if you do. I'll let you into a secret, though. To date, the only ones in your position who have ever changed their minds are men." We both had a quiet chuckle. It lightened the mood and gave me heart all at the same time.

"There *is* one thing I have changed my mind about, though," I ventured. "I realize I have said no to the L pill."

Ever a step ahead, Vera answered calmly, "I wondered whether you might. I brought the tablet with me in case you revised that opinion." She pulled it from her pocket, and I quickly took it and poked it down into the top of my outer breast pocket, where my stiletto knife was stashed.

"I could use it on the enemy, if I need to escape," I said, using this as my reason to secure it. This was my only chance to do so. While Benzedrine was flown in with the other supplies and I could get more if needed, the L pill—once declined—stayed in England.

It wasn't long before we stepped out of the staff car to find ourselves beside the Liberator. It was a generously proportioned bomber; I felt very small beside it. Some people nearby were carrying my parachute, jump helmet and goggles, the last items I would need. A tall man walked toward us, extending his hand to me for a shake.

"Ma'am, I am pleased to meet you. I'm Jerome Crance, your skipper this evening," he said in his warm, slow American accent.

"Pleased to meet you, too," I responded automatically.

Crance turned to Vera and gave her a quick "Ma'am" before continuing. "We have a large crew—you won't be meeting them all personally, but please let me introduce you both to our engineer Jose Morales, who is also your dispatcher tonight."

Another hand extended; another handshake.

A huddle formed: me, Vera, a couple of the British men who were readying me and the aircraft, and some of the Americans. Maps were reviewed, and conversations were had about drop zones and looking for lights from the reception committee on the ground.

"Let's hope for improving weather as we fly south," was Captain Crance's final statement before turning to me. "You look like you're ready to go, Miss Lampooner." I guess I was.

By now the crew had all assembled by the entry door of the bomber at the back of the aircraft; I joined them as they started to board. Turning to Vera, I met her eyes in silence. It was a weighty moment, and saying anything was beyond me.

Vera broke the silence. "Go well, Pippa." I could see her eyes brimming with tears, and bit my tongue as my throat tightened. Vera put her hands on my shoulders and uttered the traditional farewell that she bade all her girls.

"*Merde!*" French for "Shit."

We smiled, hugged, and I turned to enter the aircraft. My time had come.

SEVEN

HELLO, FRANCE

INSIDE THE LIBERATOR, THE DISPATCHER SHOWED ME where to sit on the long bench that ran along the inside of the fuselage. Behind a curtain I could see various containers, presumably also destined to be dropped into France.

"Yes, we have twelve containers and eight packages to go with you," said the dispatcher, noticing my glance. "We also have a leaflet drop to do along the way."

Within minutes the engines thundered into life and I was left alone with my thoughts as the crew busied themselves with their tasks. As the wheels left the ground, I couldn't help but think, "You're a damn fool to do this." All day I had buried that thought, but now it was there, front and center in my mind, as the tangible bump of the "wheels up" moment reminded me that I was leaving England with no guarantee of ever coming back. I was scared; no two ways about it.

Soon after takeoff the dispatcher came up close to talk to me over the constant noise of the engines.

"It's 11:40 P.M., Miss Lampooner. We have you leaving England on the first of May and arriving in France on the second. It's not a long trip—maybe an hour and a half from here to the drop zone."

I nodded. His friendly, polite, and useful communication was taking my mind away from the anxious thoughts that had so unwelcomely entered it. To occupy my mind with something else, I concentrated on watching the crew do their work. They obviously knew each other well and were cheerful and upbeat with each other, all the while efficiently performing their tasks to get their trusty aircraft to altitude. I took my cue from them, and after a few minutes started feeling better. I even had a sense of excitement.

Just as we came over the French coast the flak started and I felt the aircraft move. "Flak"—a shortened version of the German word for antiaircraft gun—referred to the artillery aimed at us from the enemy on the ground. The dispatcher was quick to dispel my concerns: "Oh, they're just pop guns, nothing for you to worry about." As the dispatcher seemed relaxed about the flak, and had the experience to know when to worry and when not to, I took his direction and ignored the "pop guns."

The Liberator's flight report, filed after the event, noted "flak observed at Bayeaux at 0204, not firing at our aircraft." That meant they got flak on the way back after my drop as well as before it; clearly this part of the French coast was a hot spot. And this fiercely protected northern coastal area was where I would be working.

Before long, containers were being shifted in readiness to drop leaflets, which were then dropped over Balleroy. Leaflet drops were common in wartime—a war of words, literally. They had two main purposes—to drop propaganda and to try to disguise the real purpose of the flight. A leaflet drop could provide an explanation for the presence of an aircraft in the vicinity, and hopefully the parachuting of an agent would be missed.

My time was coming near, and the dispatcher motioned me toward the drop area as we started getting closer to the drop zone at Mont du Saule, near Hardanges.

"Looks like the weather is on our side this trip," he said. "In the last week we've not been able to complete a couple of missions—one was due to weather, but the other one we couldn't confirm the reception on the ground. But I'm pretty sure they'll be there for you though, being a Joe and all."

A "Joe" or "J" was personnel; it was the first time the Crance crew had had a "J" on their inventory list—and a female one at that. Other times they'd had C (drop containers from the bomb bay); P, meaning packages; N for nickels, meaning propaganda leaflet bundles; and Pigeon, which denoted a wire hamper containing up to eight pigeons and fitted with a parachute. We had all but the pigeons on board Liberator 077 this night.

The all-clear signal came from the ground—flashlights, as it was too dangerous to light a bonfire in this area—and the bomber took a first run at the target, dropping the containers. The next run, to drop packages, did not eventuate, however. There was now no light signal from the ground—which meant that the Gestapo were on the move in the below villages. They would have heard the bomber and would be getting ready to check all of the farms to find out who was missing. Any military personnel in the area would also have been alerted to be on the lookout for dropped cargo—human or otherwise.

The call was made to forget about the remaining packages and deliver the human cargo before the people on the ground had to scramble back to their farms to be accounted for when the Gestapo stopped by.

In the last few minutes, something touching happened; I will always remember it. In turn, all nine crew members came in from their various stations and kissed me—quietly and without fanfare—on the forehead. I was indeed a precious cargo for them.

★ ★ ★

AS I SAT BESIDE the hole in the aircraft, ready to go with all of the predrop checks done, those annoying questioning thoughts reentered my head. "Why am I doing this?" I found myself thinking. Although I knew I could change my mind right up until I jumped, it was really too late now and I reminded myself—again—that I had been trained to do the job. I put out of my mind the thought of the men in this area who were "no longer at their posts." I needed to control my thoughts, focus on the here and now and my own ability.

In minutes I would be saying goodbye as Lampooner (Miss Lampooner to my new American friends), and landing on French soil as Plus Fours. The change of name was intended to expose double agents back in England. The Gestapo had been waiting at SOE drop zones and shooting the agents as they floated down by parachute; obviously there was a leak somewhere at the English end. Agents now went over with one name and changed it as soon as they got there. Any double agent would only ever know the English name; the French would only ever know the French one.

I also had a different field name—unknown to me—with which they would identify me back at home base in England. This name was used solely by Baker Street; none of the people in France would know it either. After the war, I found out that my field name was Geneviève. In the fifth century there had been a young girl named Geneviève who was said to have saved Paris by diverting Attila's Huns away from the city. She later became Saint Geneviève, the patron saint of Paris. Perhaps the person who named me Geneviève unconsciously had high hopes for me. The weather was now deteriorating, with ground fog swirling around, but we needed to look for an area reasonably close to the dropped containers for my own drop so that the reception committee had a decent chance of finding me. We did another couple of runs to look for a field with livestock in— many fields had been mined by the Germans, so those being grazed by animals were the only safe ones. The third pass identified a field with a few white blobs in it.

"Miss Lampooner, we think they're goats," came the call from the dispatcher. "We can drop you in that field on the next pass." Although it was a statement rather than a question, I answered anyway, in case he was wondering if I was still happy to jump.

"I grew up with goats. Okay—I'll go."

Moving to the jump position, I looked up at the light above me, waiting for it to change as the signal to exit the aircraft—rather than staring down at the open hole below me. The dispatcher motioned to me to look at him instead—which I did just as he shouted, "Go!" I pushed myself forward, through the hole, into the night sky, immediately feeling a rush of bracing cold air on my face. I felt the reassuring pull of the static line from the aircraft, opening my parachute almost immediately. We were flying at a low level, about five or six hundred feet, and I knew I would be on the ground within thirty seconds or so, which would reduce the chances of me being spotted in the moonlight. The fall was very brief, and before I knew it I could see the ground approaching below me.

* * *

I WAS HAPPY WITH the way I landed—in an open space—but the wind was troublesome and blew my parachute toward a nearby tree, dragging me along with it. What bad luck, I thought, as there seemed to be no other trees around. I managed to keep my feet on the ground but unfortunately the parachute ended up stuck in the upper branches of an apple tree.

I was trying to dislodge it when something more pressing got my attention. Hearing a scuffle behind me, I turned to face the noise. A cow had come out of the slightly foggy darkness and was staring straight at me. I was dead scared of anything with horns, and had visions of it ramming me while I was immobilized. I grabbed my Sten machine gun and pointed it at the cow, saying, "Go, go!" It's a large gun and it had the desired effect: the cow recoiled immediately. But then it lowered its head as if to charge at me. Or it could have been submission—I couldn't tell. I love animals, and my reaction to this was not one of panic but of concern for the welfare of the cow—"Oh," I thought immediately, "the poor beast must have been beaten by a stick by someone."

Slowly, carefully, I put the gun away so as not to look threatening, and then bent down and picked a large bunch of grass. I'm really not quite sure what was going through my mind, but it was innate in me to side with the animal and look friendly. By now the cow was just calmly studying me, a definite improvement.

As my attempts to pull the parachute out of the apple tree were to no avail, I needed to get my stiletto knife out of my breast pocket so that I could cut the cords. It did cross my mind that it could also be useful if the cow changed her mind and did charge at me. While the male agents were issued with larger knives, the stiletto knife for female agents looked more like a paper knife. But we had been trained how to use it if we needed to—although petite, in the right hands it could be very unkind to the recipient. As I pulled the knife out, I saw the small L pill package that I had tucked into the pocket at the last minute pop out and disappear into the darkness somewhere by my feet. As I bent down to attempt to look for it, the cow startled suddenly—not at me, but at a noise behind me. I spun around to see a young man walking up to me. He looked about seventeen, and his clothing showed that he might have come from a nearby farm. Part of the reception committee, then. After silently pointing up at my parachute, he gave it a good tug, which brought it tumbling to the ground. Next, he came over to get my overalls and headgear, presumably to bundle it all up together to dispose of. Up until now neither of us had said a word, but my removing of the overalls brought a surprised gasp from him.

"Une fille! Tu es une fille!" ("A girl! You are a girl!")

"Oui, je suis une fille," I instantly replied. ("Yes, I am a girl.")

With the initial shock of the gender of this parachutist dealt with, he introduced himself as Étienne and told me—in French, of course—that we needed to move fast. "I need to get home quickly. The Gestapo will be gathering at the gendarmerie [police station] to start checking the farms. I have to be back in my bed when they get to mine."

As Étienne was folding up the parachute, I told him that it needed to be taken to a certain person, giving him the name I'd been told at

Orchard Court. Étienne nodded to acknowledge that he knew him. "Dr. Janvier, oui. Don't worry about your equipment. I will deal with it all." He explained that it would be hidden under a hedge for now, along with my other gear, and he had everything organized.

There were, plainly, other people out of sight who had come to deal with the container drop, and Étienne would know what the wider plan was. It was not my job to worry about all that. My priority now, with Étienne's help, was to get out of the woods to a safe house before the Germans started searching the drop zone, the local villages, and the surrounding farmhouses.

As I pulled my boots off and put my French shoes on, I saw Étienne look at my boots. "May I keep them?" he asked.

"Will that not be dangerous for you, to have them in your possession?" I queried in return.

Étienne did not answer directly, but simply said they would provide good money for his household, which they sorely needed. Once again, it was not something for me to be concerned about; I was in the hands of people who were experienced at doing this. I handed them over. He smiled and seemed most grateful.

While Étienne was hiding my equipment, I ran my hands along the ground where I thought the L pill had dropped, but could not feel anything that could be that little package. While the cow had now gone, I fervently hoped that it wouldn't be curious enough to return and to eat it. Imagine if I killed an innocent animal—the thought horrified me. And, of course, the loss of the L pill also meant the loss of a swift, merciful death for me if I ever found myself in a grim situation. How foolish I had been—I should have just accepted the tablet when it was first offered and stashed it safely away like everybody else did. Had I thought I was somehow "better" than them and would not need it? How naive I had been. Still, it was one less thing to think about—which, I reminded myself, had been my original thinking around refusing it—so I was really just back to square one.

* * *

ÉTIENNE RETURNED, SNAPPING ME out of my merry-go-round of thoughts as he provided instructions about where I needed to go next. We both needed to get out of there quickly, but it would not be as a team. I was to cross the forest alone and someone else—he wasn't sure who—would meet me at the other side. The forest was divided by a road, and one section of forest was very, very thick and had German soldiers stationed there—I should avoid that area. We were in the other, much sparser section, so I would be able to travel quickly with the moonlight helping me to find my way. He pointed in the direction I needed to go and then briefly listed various landmarks to look out for on what he described as a fifteen-minute walk.

"Look for the fallen trees about five minutes in, and be careful a bit farther on because there's a dip—someone recently sprained their ankle when they fell over there. Keep on going and you'll get to your next contact." It seemed a very loose brief, but he was clearly confident that the sparse information he was giving me would suffice. And then he gave a cheery wave and was promptly swallowed up by the darkness, taking my boots with him.

I pulled out my compass, noted the direction Étienne had pointed me in, and set off. It was nerve-wracking walking among the trees alone. A woman dressed in a mustard-yellow French suit, complete with Sten gun and revolver—how could I possibly explain any of this to a German soldier? Clearly I could not, so it was best that I avoid them.

Although without a watch I could only estimate how long I'd been walking, I soon reached—without incident—what looked like the right place. Not too far away, I could make out the shape of a man leaning against a bank in the shadows. I walked on, and he came out into the moonlight. And I thought: no, it can't be.

"You?!" I exclaimed.

"Yes, it is me. Did you expect I would be staying back in England?" came the somewhat patronizing reply.

I didn't know whether I expected Claude de Baissac to be anywhere, to be honest. I knew he had spent quite some time in France and was well known in SOE circles as the organizer of the original Scientist network in Bordeaux—I had been made aware of this when I met him at my SOE interviews. But I had no idea what he had been up to since then. Why should I have?

From his sharp reaction, I wondered whether Claude had expected me to have been briefed that he was running the show and was annoyed that I hadn't been. Well, in hindsight it was probably better this way. As I was soon to discover, de Baissac was thought to be one of F Section's most difficult characters. During his training, several instructors apparently noted his volatile nature and stubborn single-mindedness.

I had thought Claude de Baissac somewhat difficult and dismissive when I had first interacted with him at Orchard Court, and suspected that his demeanor would not have changed. Indeed, in the middle of the night he looked even less happy to be around me.

"You're two hours late," he grumbled, "and our contact is waiting for us."

I was not going to wear the responsibility for that. "Blame the weather, don't blame me," I immediately said.

Claude walked over to a bicycle nestled behind a tree. The rest of our journey was to be by bike, but there was just the one and we would have to double up on it. What a cozy start with such a frosty man. He jumped onto the main seat, meaning that I'd be on the back carrier seat, which (of course) had no cushioning.

As he went to grab my Sten gun, I said, "No. I want to keep that."

"Not now you won't—give it here; no conversation."

Granted, it was easier riding for us that way—the gun was cumbersome—but his manner seemed unnecessarily curt. I gave him the Sten gun, keeping the revolver on me, and got astride the carrier seat.

We bumped along back-country lanes for what would have been about twenty minutes, I think, at a decent speed. I had no idea how far we were going, because (of course) he had not told me. We rode in silence, apart from another homily concerning the lateness of my arrival.

"Because you are late, there will now probably be a patrol coming through. At the house you are going to, where your contact is, there will likely be a German officer at the front door alcove waiting to join his patrol, so you need to avoid that."

Once in the village, Claude stopped the bike far enough away not to be seen. He gave me back my Sten gun, pointed to a group of buildings and announced that my next contact was "over there" in a house—but now, obviously, I would have to wait for the all clear to tell me there were no patrols going through.

"Okay, right," I said. "Where do I wait?"

"There's a very good tree there. Stand behind it and wait for a signal."

"But what will the signal be?" I asked his fast-disappearing back. He turned, eyeballed me, shrugged his shoulders, and said, "How should I know?"—and kept walking. Very helpful. I was on my own.

* * *

FROM BEHIND THE SUGGESTED "very good tree," I studied the buildings on the road de Baissac had pointed to. They mostly looked to be private houses—maybe six or eight of them, all at different angles (a bit higgledy-piggledy)—sitting just before the road turned a corner at the bottom. As one of the front doors of the houses opened briefly and then closed again after letting someone out, the sound of a crying baby carried through the quiet night. I froze. The light had shown a woman holding the baby—and a German soldier and an officer waiting outside the front door in the darkness, presumably to join the patrol when it came past. The door had opened for a Frenchman to come outside to have a cigarette with them. Without the baby and the light, I would not have seen the Germans. It was clearly a signal for me to stay put. About ten minutes later the patrol arrived and the two Germans joined them, falling into line as the group marched off. The Frenchman stubbed out what remained of his cigarette and went back indoors. There was nothing that I could interpret as a signal to move, so I stayed where I was and waited to see what would happen next. I could hear the marching of the patrol—there were no other noises at that time of night—and when it stopped, though in the distance, out of my sight, I continued to wait. "Watch and wait" would be something I would do a lot of in the coming months.

After a few more minutes, I heard the marching start up again and move away through a different part of town. I watched the little house intently. I felt certain that this was my contact and the man coming out with the cigarette had only done that for my benefit. There would, surely, be another signal.

Suddenly, a side door that faced my direction opened and shut three times in very quick succession. This had to be my signal; I ran there immediately. The door opened as soon as I arrived and the woman who had had the baby in her arms earlier now pulled me inside quickly. The house was as dark inside as it was outside. I was led into the next-door room, away from the windows facing onto the street, and the door was shut behind me.

This room had a little lamp in the corner; it looked comfortable and homely. Immediately there was a delighted shriek as the woman called out to the Frenchman I had seen earlier: "Salut, Paul—c'est une fille!" ("Hey, Paul—it's a girl!")

"Oh merveilleux!" ("Oh wonderful!") the man said as he, too, entered the room.

He was Dr. Paul Janvier, head of the Navarre Resistance network in the Mayenne area—the contact Buckmaster had told me about.

"Et voici Simone Baguenard," he said, "la mère du bébé qui pleure, chez qui nous sommes." ("And this is Simone Baguenard, the mother of the crying baby, whose house we are in.")

She gave me a warm, knowing smile as she added "Un bébé 'malade' que je me suis réveillé pour faire pleurer afin que vous re-gardiez dans notre direction, et qui est maintenant de retour au lit, endormi et se sentant parfaitement bien!"—"An 'unwell' baby that

I woke up to make cry so you would look our way, and who is now back in bed asleep feeling absolutely fine!"

As they both hugged and kissed me, it was not lost on me that their warm reception and sincere enthusiasm to meet me were as different as could be from Claude's manner. I felt relief. If *these* people were my trusted contacts, things were going to be alright. I was not to stay there, though, as Paul explained to me. "I have been here on a 'doctor's call' to tend to Simone's baby, and now I must return to my home in the neighboring village. You will come with me."

Paul's trusty Simca was parked around the back of the house, away from any prying eyes. As I scrambled into the back of the car, under a blanket and nestled in with various medical bags, he assured me that it would be a short trip and he would be unlikely to be stopped. Any German patrol seeing him would know he was just doing his job as the local doctor in the area. His profession meant that he was one of the rare people to have a car and be allowed to use it; being on the road at night was quite normal for a doctor.

I would later find out that the name of Simone's village was Champgenéteux and Paul had his home and medical practice almost four and a half miles away in Bais. The road signs had been removed by the Germans, but of course the locals knew where they were going. It was, as Paul had said, a quick trip with nobody stopping us. There was nothing more for me to do tonight; Paul showed me a bedroom and suggested I get some sleep. The following day we would make plans for what came next. Up until now the flow of adrenaline had kept me from feeling tired, but the crazy twenty-four hours that had just passed were catching up with me and I suddenly felt a wave of exhaustion.

The duck-down duvet enveloped me like a fluffy cloud. It felt heavenly. As I lay waiting for sleep to come, it seemed a very long time ago that I had woken in Orchard Court. "Well, it's over. I'm here," I thought, pleased that my arrival was behind me. Of course, although the drop was over and I had connected with the Scientist network and found my French contact on the ground, my journey was far from over. It was only just beginning.

EIGHT

A NEW IDENTITY

I HAD NO SOONER WOKEN UP THE NEXT DAY WHEN A kind-looking woman arrived with a tray of food. I must have been in a deep slumber because I had a moment of not thinking clearly and addressed her in English: "Good morning, thank you for this." Perhaps I had woken mid-dream, for in that moment I thought I was in London and even said so. She told me I was in France. Of course I was. I was at the doctor's house, and this was his house-keeper. That would be the last English I spoke for some time.

I devoured my breakfast—albeit at lunchtime, when I woke—complete with "coffee" made from burned barley, without sugar or milk. It was the beginning of a diet that was going to be anything but normal. I was used to rations, but living on the move, as my job would require of me now, would make trying to get enough nutritious food rather challenging. I was already quite light at a hundred pounds.

After breakfast, Paul asked to look at my papers.

"You are twenty-nine years old? Born in 1915?" he questioned, in French of course. I would always speak French from now on.

"No," I replied, shaking my head. "I am twenty-three years old and born in 1921." At least the date of April 8 was right—the best alias stories and names had a portion of truth in them, which helped you to remember.

Paul shook his own head, signaling his disbelief, I think, that the people in England could ever have thought I could pass for a twenty-nine-year-old. He promptly asked Paulette Pelletier, his longstanding employee at his surgery, to go and find a certain person and bring him back. After she headed off, Paul told me he trusted her completely and she was extremely helpful, but lately he had been a little worried that her calm ability to accept the comings and goings of strange people might compromise her if she was ever questioned.

"I must protect her from some things," he said. "Trust is problematic in wartime. Simone Baguenard, who you met last night, does not even share what she does for the Resistance cause with her own sister, who lives a few doors down from her across the road. People often don't trust their own family, their friends, or their neighbors."

I took the opportunity to ask Paul about two other people London had told me I could trust—giving him their numbers only, not their names. Paul confirmed that both, one a grocer and the other a vet, would be available if I needed them. He described the vet as a kindly man who had ended up giving a home to the many unwanted dachshund dogs the French were getting rid of. I thought how sad it was that these dogs were also a casualty of war—they had done nothing wrong except have a German breed name. War is so stupid. I am quite sure the dogs had no animosity toward any human regardless of their nationality. I immediately liked the sound of the vet. The Germans liked him too, apparently, because they saw he chose to collect German dogs!

* * *

IT WASN'T LONG BEFORE Paulette returned—along with a man with a camera, who took my photo and then left. Paul told me—as I suspected—that I was going to get new identity papers and should never use what I had been given in England. His plan was for me to take on the persona of a fourteen-year-old. This was quite startling. Although I knew I looked younger than my years, why would he make me as young as fourteen, rather than perhaps sixteen or seventeen? The answer was sobering: it was to save me facing the same fate as local Resistance members. The Germans were sending boys as young as fifteen years old to Germany to do forced labor, and there was the very real possibility they might soon start on the girls.

My story was to be that I had been at school in Paris, but it had to close because of the war and all the girls got sent back to their parents. I had no way to get back to the Belgian Congo, which was where I was from. I liked this: I could easily talk about my schooling in Africa if the Germans wanted to check whether those places existed, which of course they did. Paul didn't think they would do any more than check the name of a school—getting a school roll out of Africa would be far too difficult.

Because I could not get back to Africa, I was instead sent to northern France to live with my grandparents and help them on their little farm in Champgenéteux. They made soap from the milk of the goats they owned, and I was to pedal my bike around the area to sell the soap and bring in a small income. Paul said he had an older couple in mind whom he felt would be perfect for the job. The story would go that they had friends in other villages who could also do with my help selling their goat's milk soap. This cover story would allow me to cycle from place to place, picking up soap, selling it, then returning to the various farms with the money I'd gathered, to pick up more soap and continue my travels about the area. It was the perfect cover for a secret agent needing to gather information on troop movements and other facts that London might find useful. Paul suggested that my clientele would likely even include the German soldiers themselves!

Next, we needed a name for this teenage soap-seller. Paul asked me about my schooling in Paris, and I told him about a girl (younger than me) called Paulette who had attended at the same time I was there. Her surname was only slightly different from mine—it was de Latour, not Latour. Paulette de Latour was Swiss, while Phyllis Latour was from Africa. Paul thought this extremely useful and that I should assume her identity. I suggested adding in Jeannine as a middle name—it was a sentimental thing for me to have my godmother always with me, and Paul did not see it as an issue. Now, if the Germans were to check, there would be a pupil on the school roll who had the exact same first and last names as what was on my new papers.

When it came to age, though, Paulette would still be nearer my actual age than the fourteen Paul wanted for me. However, he thought that fourteen would still be okay because everything else matched and the Germans would just be looking for the name on a school roll. If they noticed that the year was wrong, it could easily be passed off as an error. Given that I could genuinely talk about being schooled at that particular school in Paris, Paul was confident I could pull this off if I was ever asked about it. He wasn't concerned about the school having by now been shut down for quite a while, or the way in which this had happened.

So, it was settled. I felt excited about this new existence. I had loved being young and carefree as a teenager, so this new persona was far more akin to a role I could genuinely and confidently play—rather than being a stuffy secretary of twenty-nine, which was something I had no knowledge of. In any case, the original "older secretary from Lyon" cover story dreamed up by London—with no consultation with me—had me indulging my love of bird-watching to give me an excuse for traveling. I am not at all sure that this hasty idea would have worked, as I could not have brought a camera or binoculars with me. Thank goodness that Paul thought things through properly and came up with a more plausible story.

Of course, we did not contact the real Paulette in Switzerland then—in wartime, the less said the better. We took our chances that she would not be back in France. I did, however, get in touch with her parents postwar and tell them what I had done. A long time after the war, I was awarded parachute wings by a French parachuting regiment. I absolutely loved having the wings, but the certificate that came with them had "de Latour" on it rather than "Latour." It was an easy mistake to make, in the circumstances.

I made my own mistake, too, by failing to inform London of my new identity—which caused quite some problems later on. However, in my defense my mind was keenly focused on getting going and it simply did not occur to me to let London know of the changed arrangements for me on the ground.

My new identity papers would likely be with me by the next day; until then, I could not leave the confines of Paul's house.

★ ★ ★

OUR CONVERSATION TURNED TO the English agents on the ground and how they and the French worked together. Paul told me that the message about my arrival had been heard on the BBC a few days ago: "Le vin rouge est le meilleur"—"Red wine is the best." It had been repeated yesterday, which meant I would arrive that night. Radio Londres had done its job.

Being with the forces of the Free French, Paul explained, he took direction from the French despite working closely with SOE. I had been advised in London that the various political and Resistance factions in France were complicated, overlaid by tension between the English and the French resistance organizations on the ground. I understood that to mean that I should take my own counsel and make my own judgments on who I could, or could not, trust. Trying to work out the politics of it all was really hard, not to say exhausting—who were partisans, who were communists, who were collaborators and double agents; who were Free France de Gaullists, who were Maquis, who were Francs-Tireurs et Partisans (FTP—an armed Resistance organization created by leaders of the French Communist Party, although you didn't have to be a communist to join), etc., etc. Looking back now, I recall that on the French side of things it was really the communists whom I could mostly trust. And of course Paul (not a communist) was trustworthy—I knew that to be a fact already, and I knew that Simone would be, too, because Paul trusted her.

Trust is one thing; quite another who you take direction from, and who gets on with who. I felt that Paul was subtly reminding me that although he was working alongside SOE, he remained under the military orders of the French. Perhaps that was because he had Claude de Baissac to deal with. Claude had his own thoughts on how things should be done—things that suited Claude's own agenda—and I found myself wondering how all of this was going to pan out. Paul respected Charles de Gaulle, in exile in England, but you could not say the same of Claude. He was not a fan of de Gaulle, and de Gaulle himself was not a great fan of SOE. Even though ending the war was a shared goal, a lot of the time how you got there wasn't a shared ethos. It was all really complicated.

In my mind, I had decided I would only be using Scientist (the network run by Claude) as a backup group. As soon as I was given a courier, I would be gone. Hopefully I would not have much to do with Claude directly—that's what couriers were for. I would stick to myself on the road and quietly blend in as I observed daily goings-on.

There was, however, to be more contact than that. Paul told me that I was to connect with Claude later that evening. He explained how Claude had turned up at his house on April 10—not even a month ago—accompanied by another SOE agent. Frenchman Jean Renaud-Dandicolle was known by his field name of René. His papers from his training in England have his alias as Jean-Marie Demirmont and his code name was Verger. The two men made it clear to Paul that SOE's Buckmaster in London had charged de Baissac with building up the Resistance in this area (with René as his second-in-charge), with the task of organizing the necessary equipment and weaponry that needed to be parachuted in from England and dispersed. It was an open secret that an Allied coastal invasion was looming, and the Normandy coast was going to be contested ground.

Paul had accommodated the men initially, but felt it more prudent to move them to a small, abandoned farm, La Roisière in

Champgenéteux, which belonged to his mother—she owned three farms locally. When I met Paul's mother a few weeks later, I was surprised at how young she looked. In all the time I was there I only met her three or four times, because Paul liked to keep her out of things. She was very much in the background. I would later find out that she was happy to help me with hiding radio sets and had also hidden Jewish people, so it was a situation of "like mother, like son."

It has to be said that just because people were related to each other, you could never assume they shared the same politics and beliefs, or had any knowledge of the clandestine war efforts supposedly going on under their noses. Simone's sister never knowing of Simone's work in the Resistance was a great example. Keeping things to yourself was a good way to protect other people. If they weren't told anything, they wouldn't know anything if they were asked. The less people knew, the better. Tight was good. Another example of this was close to home for me. The morning after my arrival, nearby people would turn up at dawn to use their horses only to find the animals exhausted and sweaty; they might wonder who hadn't told them what was going on—or perhaps they felt it was better not to know! The reception teams from the villages of Hambers and Bais, who had met my drop, had "borrowed" horses for a high-speed round trip of some nineteen miles overnight, to move the containers. They hid the dropped equipment in some sheds at Marche and put the horses back in their paddocks at about 4 A.M. It had been a very busy night for those horses.

★ ★ ★

A KNOCK ON THE door was followed by a familiar face. Simone, the mother with the crying baby, had come back to get a "check-up" for her supposedly unwell seven-month-old son. Having a doctor's practice meant a lot of people coming and going for appointments, so it was the perfect cover for appointments of a nonmedical nature, too.

There was something instantly likable about Simone. I looked at the bonny wee baby boy in her arms and asked how he was.

"He's feeling much better now," she said with a knowing smile. We shared a chuckle.

Simone and her husband, Georges, the local grocer in Champgenéteux, were well involved in the goings-on, and Paul had told Claude and René that the couple could have the transmitter at their house in Champgenéteux on occasion to take advantage of the power connected up there and save us having to always pedal to recharge the batteries.

As a local, Simone could travel around the immediate area without needing a cover story. She told me that Paul would always know where she was likely to be, so anytime I was back in Bais he would be a good person to connect with to pass information through. If she and I were both traveling, we would try to meet elsewhere. That way she could pass me any information she thought useful to pass on to London, and I could pass pertinent information to her to bring back to Claude, Paul, and the others on the ground here. We were never to be seen together in one place meeting regularly, regardless of where it was. And if I was to ever meet her at the practice, it was only ever to be at night. In fact, I would need to meet even Paul—anyone, really—at night. That was the safest way.

I felt that Simone was the perfect person with whom to leave my gold SOE items from Buckmaster and Vera Atkins. They were certainly *not* traveling with me. I explained to her how I hoped I would never need to sell them, but rather would be coming back to get them at the end of this awful war. As I handed her my gold compact and pen, I felt sure that I would see them again—how joyous that day would be. It was beyond my imagination to think about it being a reality, but in my heart I felt it was within reach. The Allies would soon have Jerry on the run, surely?

* * *

SOON AFTER MY NEW identity paperwork arrived, I was presented with some clothes to try on—something more appropriate than the mustard secretary suit. There was a plain little blue dress that looked like it had seen better days, and what looked like a typical sort of school uniform, which I would wear meeting my pseudo-grandparents in the coming days. The outfit came with some simple lace-up shoes, but no cardigan or jacket. Mind you, it was almost summer, so hopefully I wouldn't need one. I tried on the clothes and they fitted well.

I would be meeting my "grandparents" in public so that anyone who was watching (either openly or sneakily) would be made aware of the situation we had cooked up. But for us to meet authentically as people who knew each other, we both needed to know what the other party looked like and get our story straight. The couple therefore had an "appointment" at Paul's surgery first thing this morning.

Monsieur and Madame Durand looked like good people. At the time I thought they looked old, but they were probably only in their sixties. They told me they had a daughter who had separated from her husband some time back and was often at their home visiting. She was trustworthy. Paul went through my story again with me, and for the first time with them, working out some practicalities as we went. He told me never to be tempted to hide in the attic if the house was searched by the Germans. After speaking to everyone in the house, they would usually fire a few rounds up into the ceiling as they left, to make sure they hadn't missed anyone hiding up there. People had died this way, so it was good information to know.

If this rattled my "grandparents," they did not show it. They were so brave—they were helping a secret agent in plain sight of a German officer who was billeted in their house. We would all have to be extremely careful.

After farewelling the Durands until Paul could orchestrate our reunion, I set about the task of hiding my codes. The codes were all on a piece of silk, and that piece of silk needed to be hidden well. If it was to be found it would be a dead giveaway—"dead" being the operative word. There would be no mercy, no way out, for me. Secret agents were dealt with harshly and we all knew it. I had asked Paul for some knitting needles, a big ball of wool, and a little bag to put it all in. The piece of silk was five square inches and weighed very little. My shoelaces were flat, formed from a woven tube rather than a cord, and my idea was to cut the ends off a spare shoelace and push the silk into it using the knitting needle. I would use the shoelace as a tie for my hair, which was not an unusual thing to do given the lack of money around wartime France. It was a perfectly sensible use of an everyday item.

I tested it out. It looked good enough, I thought, but needed a bit more disguising around the ends of the lace. I set to knitting a couple of pompoms and attached them at either end of the shoelace, leaving a tiny gap so that the silk could be pushed in and pulled out from underneath the pompom. I was happy with my handiwork—it looked like something a fourteen-year-old would wear and was a nifty solution for hiding my codes. Every time I used a code I would have to prick it so I knew it had been used, and having a pin along with wool, knitting, and needles all went together very nicely. I was rather pleased with myself as I knitted a few inches of a scarf to make it all seem legitimate, then set everything aside as an important job done.

The theater of connecting with my "grandparents" in public was played out successfully as we made our happiness at the reunion evident. "It was a long trip from Paris—we have your room ready" sort of thing. Hugs all round, and talk about having the soap all ready to sell. I have to say it was good to see daylight again after being cooped up in Paul's place. The Durands' house on their little farm on the outskirts of Champgenéteux looked homely, as I had expected it would, with a lovely garden that was obviously their pride and joy. I also met the trustworthy daughter they had mentioned, who "just happened" to be visiting that day. The Durands' billeted German officer was not there when I arrived, so I quickly took the opportunity to use the radio set secreted away there to let home base know I had arrived safely.

It was to be message number one on day two of an unknown number of messages and days stretching ahead of me.

Before too long I was on my bike and on the road, getting to know my environment. It was not unusual to see a girl on a bicycle in France, and I did not feel conspicuous. It was also not strange that I would not be staying the night there, because I was the helpful granddaughter keen to be off selling soap and would be staying with other people known to my grandparents. The Germans had removed or painted out the street signs and village names, so my visual memory needed to be attuned. Thankfully I had very sharp recall, almost photographic for some things.

★ ★ ★

THAT NIGHT I WAS back at Paul's house to meet Claude, who needed to brief me on two matters—what was to happen next, and a little knowledge of the people involved in the Scientist network. The most pressing need was to get me out on the road in the morning, with René, to familiarize me with the area I would be working in, and to get to know where the sets were located. Unlike static radio operators with a fixed set in one place, I would be traveling the coastal area, covering over sixty miles, and using multiple sets hidden in various places north and west of Caen toward the Saint-Lô area. René (or Verger) was an experienced courier, described to me by Claude as his long-serving lieutenant.

René would be looking after the northern half of the area, including north of Caen, where I would be working. Maurice Larcher (code name Vladimir), who was also known as Linesman or Maurice Langlade, was another radio operator; he would be focusing on the area to the south and east, with Claude. Claude said that he would have to move around quite a lot to keep ahead of the Gestapo and to be across the breadth of activity he felt was needed at this point in the war.

He finished by mentioning that there were two female couriers as well, one being his sister Lise de Baissac and the other a Russian called Katia Anzi. Knowing how prickly Claude could be, I wondered if his sister would be much better. Baker Street had told me it was my choice as to who my courier was, and it sounded like there was now a choice of Lise or Katia. I thought that a woman would be good to travel with, but felt it prudent to leave that decision until after my familiarization trip with René, which was to start the next day.

It was evident from his manner that Claude plainly thought of me as the new kid and himself as the old hand who deserved some respect. Given our first interaction months ago, when I'd felt he misunderstood me, followed by the frosty reception I'd gotten from him when I arrived, I suppose the briefing could have been worse. Perhaps he was being benevolent because he was in dire need of another radio operator on the ground and London had delivered one to him extremely promptly. He had also come to realize that women were useful. He was on the record as being "against the use of women as agents because their nerves are not usually strong enough for the job," but had since seen that they were invaluable— men readily aroused suspicion and got arrested, whereas women did not.

We both knew that the three men who had previously worked the area I was going into had been caught. I presumed they were now POWs somewhere. I didn't think Scientist could have been their backup group as it was then only just re-forming. If Claude had any more information than I did, he did not proffer it. I am sure, however, that he knew what London knew—they had been killed, rather than captured. It was probably better that I was not offered that bleak information in London. I would not find it out until after the war.

Although I knew a little of Claude's history, at the time I was not aware of the minutiae of his previous trips to France. In the previous incarnation of Scientist, run by de Baissac a year before in the Bordeaux region, Claude had only managed minor successes in sabotage. He felt that this was because he did not have enough weaponry to do the job, so in his eyes, he was constrained. Scientist's intelligence work, however, received great praise. Claude's second entry to France saw him form a connection with a general in the right-wing OCM (Organisation Civile et Militaire) Resistance movement, enabling him to build a secret army of resisters, which by some accounts eventually rose to around twenty thousand men. Rather than concentrate on sabotage against rail, electricity, radio, and industrial targets, Claude preferred to focus on the organization, training, and arming of these men in guerrilla warfare. The RAF helped his cause, supplying him with huge quantities of weapons and explosives.

The momentum was not to last, however. The general involved with the OCM was arrested in Paris and identified the key Resistance people in the Scientist network to the Gestapo—meaning that huge stashes of hidden arms were uncovered. Within months Scientist had completely collapsed and Claude and his sister Lise—who had organized her own network in Poitiers and used Scientist (and other networks) for radio messages—were back in England looking for their next task in France.

It was now apparent that I was to be involved in this next task. Would this involve Claude building up another secret army in the north, wreaking havoc with sabotage, excelling with intelligence-gathering, or all three? The de Baissac energy was something special to contend with, and now I had two of them to work with. It was my understanding that Scientist would be my backup group rather than me being inside it completely. Accordingly, I decided to just stick to what I needed to do—gather intelligence in my travels, send it back to England, and try to stay out of the way of the de Baissac siblings. The following day I would meet René and start that work. I was excited.

NINE

A STRANGE NEW LIFE

I WAS EXPECTING TO MAKE CONTACT WITH RENÉ THE next morning bright and early, but it was not to be. Paul's warning about house searches proved prophetic. "Quick!" he whispered. "You need to get out, the Germans are searching homes from door to door."

Thankfully I was ready to go, and when he opened the back door a few minutes later it was to a tall, slim, dark-haired woman who gestured me quickly to follow her. This was Katia. I would later learn that although she was technically Russian, most of her life had been spent in Italy and she had Italian papers. Her parents were not Party people and had managed to get out of Russia with Katia when she was only seven years old, to start a new life in Italy. Katia was now twenty-nine and in a war zone. How and why she came to be here in France as a courier I did not ever really find out.

Katia took me into the forest, where René came out of the shadows, and we were introduced. He was a young, fresh-faced twenty-year-old, but had seen a lot of life. When France fell to the Nazis in June 1940, René had still been a schoolboy. After joining the Resistance in early 1942 he found himself working with Claude in

131

his hometown of Bordeaux for the first Scientist network. After being sought by the Gestapo, he escaped to England in August 1943. There, he was commissioned into the British Army where he trained with SOE under the pseudonym of Jean Danby. He and Claude were paired up again by SOE for Scientist 2 in Normandy, and he parachuted back into France at the end of January 1944, about three months before me.

Like mine, René's training had been shortened due to the necessity of getting people on the ground in France. His records would describe him as "very intelligent, keen, and enterprising," with one of his instructors reflecting that it was a great pity there was no time to train him fully. I liked René and had a good feeling about him. And if he was keen for a second network with Claude de Baissac in charge, then surely I must be able to get along with Claude myself. As Claude's trusted second-in-command, René had set up a lot of contacts before Claude arrived in mid-February. He would no doubt be looking to cement the ones he had and secure some more on our expedition. He was a knowledgeable person to travel with and get an understanding of the reality of my new life.

* * *

I HAD MY TRUSTY Michelin map with me, which was a very normal thing to travel with. No internet back then! With the village and street signs blacked out it was quite common to see people studying maps, wondering if they were heading in the right direction. That Michelin map was to become my best friend. I would use it to pinpoint drop zones (DZs) for parachute drops in my communications. The map was gridded, and an identical copy was kept in London. From France, we would be able to request a drop at a specific coordinate, for example DZ at G9. I would then add a nearby village to the message—like "4km NNE of Saint-Mars"—which would provide a double check to make sure both parties were literally "on the same page."

First, though, I needed to find where the sets were. I would be working in the middle of the second line of the Germans' defense, a very dangerous place to be. The area I would cover lay along the Normandy coast but not right on it. The coastal area was "Verboten"—a forbidden, all-German area. They knew that this was an obvious place for an Allied invasion of occupied Europe and had progressively tried to protect their position. In 1942, Hitler had ordered the construction of a two-thousand-mile-long chain of coastal fortifications that ran from the Franco-Spanish border to northern Norway, which became known as the Atlantic Wall. In early 1944 it was further strengthened with reinforced concrete pillboxes built on the beaches, and sometimes slightly inland, as well as along the roads leading away from the beaches. These held machine guns, anti-tank guns, and light artillery. The beaches were mined, as was the water just offshore, and obstruction beams were dug deep into the sand. Only Germans were allowed in this area, so I worked back from the coast a way.

To aid in finding the seventeen sets, before I left England I had been given some general information regarding their localities. There was a lot more that was unknown, so my first task was to locate the sets over the next two weeks with René. Once I had found them, and marked them ever so discreetly on my map, I would soon become familiar with the area and know where to go. I would never carry a set myself, just ride my bike to where one was located and use it in situ there. René knew the Normandy area well, so was the perfect person to do this familiarization task with me. When I say "with" me, though, we made sure that we were very rarely seen together on this trip.

The three farms that gave me my supplies of soap to sell were each hiding a set—including my "grandparents." These were easy to locate on the map. The fourteen others were to be found in various places over that roughly sixty-mile area, originally hidden by my three trusted contacts: Paul, the vet, and the grocer. Those in certain civilian professions, like Paul's as a doctor, were granted limited access to rationed petrol and permission to use a car if their work was considered essential. I am quite sure that Paul's reliable little Simca had been very useful for sneaking a set or two in the back along with his doctor's satchel in order to get them hidden in the right places. I wasn't sure how long ago these sets had been put there, just that the agents who had been using them were no longer here. We all knew in SOE that the job carried risks, and lots of them.

René and I set off on our bikes. It was a good hour's ride before we got to where I had deduced I needed to be. The information given to me in England included a very specific time to be at this place. I knew I simply could not be late, or I would miss my contact who was expecting me. Thankfully I was a few minutes early, according to the church bells. Not having a watch, I used church bells as my timepiece. The place I was looking for was a park. I left my bike in a rack and sighted a park bench close by. I also noticed that René, traveling some way behind me, had parked his bike some distance away and started to go for a wander.

I stood there for a few minutes, looking at the summery scene and wondering what would happen next. The church bells told me when I needed to sit on the park bench, and I did just that. Soon enough, a man walking past stopped near me.

"Is anyone else needing the bench?" he asked in French. I replied in the negative and gestured for him to sit, which he duly did. I can't remember if we exchanged any conversation or not, but if we did it would have been brief and courteous—about the weather or something innocuous like that. It wasn't long before he stood up to leave, extending his hand for a handshake in a "nice to meet you" sort of moment. As I accepted his hand, I felt a small piece of paper in his palm, which I took discreetly.

"Good day," he bade me, before striding off. We had, of course, practiced this sort of thing back in England, so it felt quite familiar. I waited there for a little while before getting up, picking up my bike and riding off, out of town. Stopping in a hidden wooded area a short way away, I examined the paper. It had a number written on it—a grid location for my Michelin map. The information gave me the location of my first set, which I discreetly marked on the map with a little dot. René's knowledge of the area had us success-fully locate it that afternoon—in some ruins—after a bit of a hunt around. By this stage of the war the sets were quite small and thus easy to hide.

Late that night, when my sked was due, we went back to try the set out. My "sked" was a prearranged time at which London expected to hear from me. Mine was originally set in the early hours of the morning, but I had succeeded in getting that changed to 11:30 P.M.

The Type 3 Mk II set (commonly known as the B2) that I used came in two alternative casings—a small suitcase for non-exposed places or a container for moist areas such as forests, where a lot of my sets were located. Both were compact and had three parts to them—the sending part at the top, the receiving part at the bottom, and the battery on the right. The three things that needed to be done so I could communicate were connecting the antenna to an antenna wire, the earth to an earth wire, and having a power supply that worked. I opened up the set, turned it on, and connected the antenna and earth wires. Due to my proximity to home base in England, I felt I would not need to get the antenna up too high and just threw it over a hedge nearby. The charged battery (care of René) did its job and it seemed like we were in business.

On the transmitter panel at the top of the set there was a switch on the left-hand side, which had three positions marked "T," "S" and "R" on it—standing for *tune* (the transmitter) and *send* or *receive* (messages). The transmission frequency was controlled by the all-important quartz crystal, which plugged into a little spot on the right-hand side. The quartz is a different thickness for different frequencies. It's a slab of quartz, a bit like a stone; if it is thinner then the frequency is higher, and if thicker then the frequency is lower. I had my own quartz crystal with me and plugged it into the allocated hole. There was another hole to plug a Morse key into—I carried my own personal one, so plugged that in too.

At the bottom of the set was the receiving side of things. Just like any radio, there was a control for tuning the receiver and another for the volume. The controller in between them (a thing called a BFO, which stands for beat frequency oscillator) allowed the incoming signal to be converted into nicely audible tones. If it was not switched on, the Morse code coming into the headphones would not be very clear.

Then it was a matter of putting my headphones on and identifying myself to London in a secure manner using Morse code. My job was then to take down what England sent to me (to decode) and to send them my encoded messages. Brevity was important because I did not want to be found doing what I was doing.

This first time, after briefly checking in with London I shut down the set and put it all to bed back where it was nicely hidden. That made two sets I had now seen and used—one where my "grandparents" lived and now this one. Just fifteen more to find!

* * *

THE NEXT DAY, AFTER a very early start and a bike ride of a couple of hours, we reached another village. Here, London had told me to go to a certain café at a certain time. This was one occasion when René and I were to be seen together.

French cafés and restaurants used to be busy places with a steady stream of people, but wartime had put paid to that. Access to food was another casualty of war. As we arrived, at the appointed time, I looked across the road at the long lines of well-dressed Frenchwomen waiting patiently outside the shops, hoping to use their ration tickets to get something to feed their families. The sad reality was that when they finally got to the front of the line, there might not be anything to buy. Ration tickets only gave you the right to stand in long lines, with no guarantee of getting anything. I looked at their concerned faces and wondered who it was they needed to feed. A child, an old person?

Although things were considerably better in the country than in the cities, given the proximity to farms, access to food had been in a dire state for the past four years. Food was scarce and things like potatoes, meat, sugar, milk, and eggs were now largely unavailable because they were being redirected to the occupying German army and to Germany itself. That left the locals with rutabaga, cabbages, and the like. Substitution became normal: butter became lard, coffee became chicory, and pâtés became meatless—prepared with flour, egg, a meat extract like Oxo, and water. Nothing was as it had been before the war.

Food for the local populace had become controlled as soon as France was occupied, and became more so as time went on. The rations were not enough to feed anyone properly. For an adult they consisted of just 12 ounces of bread a day; less than 2 ounces of cheese and 11 ounces of meat a week; and less than 2 ounces of rice, 9 ounces of pasta, 9 ounces of margarine, and 18 ounces of sugar a month. That added up to about 1,300 calories a day—about half of what you really need to function as an adult.

To survive in the big cities, people took matters into their own hands. In Paris it was said that people were breeding rabbits and guinea pigs in their bathtubs to sell as meat to neighbors, and taking trains to the country to buy a few goods from farmers to sell back in the city at a small profit. Rows upon rows of floral window boxes were transformed into vegetable patches for carrots and parsnips. Inevitably, a black market sprang up around forged or stolen ration tickets. It was a risky business, though—stealing, forging, or selling those tickets was punishable by death.

At the café, René and I ordered cold drinks and sat and watched the activities of the village, beyond the ration line. A cool drink was welcome after our early-morning bike ride of some twelve miles, but it was also a safe option for blending in with the locals. The SOE training had drummed into us not to do the English thing and put milk in before the tea, but rather follow the French custom of putting the milk in last. There were also lessons about coffee orders that could flag you as not being local—and we needed to look local.

Not long after we had taken the first welcome sips of our drinks, we saw a man come in and sit at a table not far from us. He was served by the waiter, finishing his drink soon after being served. He put his cup down, took the few steps over to our table and leaned in, signaling that he wanted to talk to us. Politely, he said he found himself to be in an unexpected hurry and, as such, would we be so kind as to pay his bill for him, if he left us the required money?

"Bien sûr [Of course]," I answered.

He briefly peered closely at his bill, as if to see what he owed, then (bill and all) put his hand in his pocket to retrieve a few francs and placed them on the table in front of us. He left with a cheery "Merci" and a tip of his hat.

We promptly got up ourselves and paid the cashier for both bills before getting on our bikes and heading out of the village.

Along with the money, the man had delivered a piece of paper much the same size as the French francs. Again, it had a number on it. That meant another set ever so discreetly marked on the Michelin map. We had now found two sets in two days, which became our norm.

* * *

IT WOULD TAKE US just under two weeks to cover the ground needed to find the locations of all the well-hidden sets. René's geographical knowledge of local roads, along with other local knowledge from the Resistance network, helped us cover a huge area of ground efficiently. Secretive connections with people providing numbers on pieces of paper were made in various places—sometimes just with René, sometimes just with me—as we filled my Michelin map with little dots. Strange people giving me information in unusual ways (and me not batting an eyelid about it) became second nature. This secretive life of random connections with people I would probably never see again passing on information that was dangerous in the wrong hands—with lethal repercussions—felt remarkably normal in quite a short amount of time.

I had a moment one day on my bike when my mind wandered to Lilian Rolfe. Having roomed with her on our first day as SOE and trained with her for a period, I knew she must now also be somewhere in France, finding her way in this perilous situation we had both been selected for and trained to try to survive. Of course I had no idea where she was, but I hoped we would both get through and be able to meet up in London as we had planned. I do wonder whether the day she landed was in fact the day I was thinking about her. Lilian landed by Lysander on May 6, 1944, just four days after I did, southwest of Paris to work with the Historian network.

My sets were hidden in a variety of places: ditches, hedges, forests, or concealed in ruinous, bombed-out buildings. With each set I took great care to examine where exactly it was, taking note of fallen or unusually shaped trees or things in the natural landscape that would sear that particular place into my brain. My photographic memory for places especially made it easy for me to lock in a visual picture and be able to readily recall it later. It was a trait of mine that proved very useful, and it has never really left me.

For the sets in ruins behind farmhouses—there were maybe four of them—the three parts (sender, receiver, and battery) were hidden separately. There might be a battery in one corner, the sending part in another, and the receiving part in yet another place. Once each had been located I would put the set together, plug in my crystal, and test that things were working—and then pull it all apart and hide the components again. Other things were routinely hidden with the sets, like Benzedrine tablets and weapons, and René and I checked that they were still there. I did not carry a gun with me, but this way I knew I could access one when needed. With each set were a revolver with a silencer, a Sten gun, and the appropriate ammunition for both. Five of the seventeen sets also had an S-Phone, which we called a "sugar phone"—a two-way ground-to-air UHF radio developed in 1942 in Britain for use by SOE and Resistance groups operating behind enemy lines. It was a way to communicate with intelligence officers in aircraft that were flying close to the occupied territory at high altitude. There was a ground unit and a matching airborne unit. I also had six bikes stashed in various places in case the one I was using became unusable for any reason.

The Michelin map was pure gold. It showed everything I needed, above and beyond villages and roads—it showed forests, ruins, ditches. Normandy was known for its huge hedges and deep ditches and overgrown landscapes with sunken roads. As, of course, there was no help to be had from a road or village sign, studying the map with its geographical features was extremely helpful for me in understanding where I was.

While the Normandy landscape was good for hiding in while preparing for D-Day, it would not—geographically speaking—be as friendly for an invasion force, as the Allies would soon find out. The area I was covering, north of Caen toward the coast, went from the vast plains near Caen to small orchards and cultivated fields bordered with hedges out west at the base of the Cotentin Peninsula. It was a lot of land to cover on a bike, with there being some nineteen miles or so between each set even though they were closer than that "as the crow flies." On this trip René and I were actively avoiding the German army, so would often zigzag about to get to the next set. Later, when I was operating in this area, I would also be zigzagging around the place but with the opposite intent—to stay close to them. When they moved, so would I.

The soap the German soldiers were issued with was like sandpaper and what I was selling was a much nicer option. It gave me the perfect opportunity to find where the German army was located and to overhear conversations. To them I was nothing but a fourteen-year-old girl trying to make some money for her family from their goats. I sold them soap, and they (unwittingly) gave me valuable information. There was no way that they could know the true price of the transaction. That small ball of velvety soap might well cost them more than sixteen cents. It might even cost them their lives once I'd called in their position and then hastily removed myself before the damage could be done from above.

* * *

RENÉ AND I WERE a good team, and those couple of weeks on the road with him helped me understand him a little better. He easily straddled the English and French worlds and was far more mature than his twenty years. War does that to you. You grow up quickly, by necessity, and see stuff that young people should never be exposed to. Well—any people really, regardless of their age. I wish I could have not seen the death and destruction that I saw in my time in France. Once you see it, it is a memory that always sits there just below the surface and may pop up anytime.

We located the two other farms where the goat's milk soap would be coming from. I was pleased to make the acquaintance of the farmers, who were communists. René did not come with me to see them. Both farms would become a regular visit for me. Each time I arrived, we would have conversations about the amount of soap being sold, the fresh soap I would need from them, and the amount of money I had managed to earn them from my travels. This initial visit, though, was just a first hello. Like my "grandparents," these farmers were both hiding radio sets. Brave patriots as they were, they knew exactly what I was doing.

On this familiarization trip René had some established contacts who provided some sleeping options for us, but I knew that when I was eventually on my own with my courier we would be sleeping outdoors and living on the road. The wonderful thing about visiting these two farmhouses and my "grandparents" was the added benefit of—sometimes—sleeping in a proper bed in a proper house. What a complete treat that was on the odd occasion I did it. Mostly, though, I just picked up the soap and left, as I did not want to put them at risk.

The sets were hidden in their stables behind the main house. Every farm (theirs included) had a German officer billeted there. While the officer was sleeping or eating, I would be busy sending messages from the stable out the back, under the premise of gathering balls of soap. Charging of the batteries would sometimes be done at the stables when the German officers were out, and up to five could be charged at one time. It would be the job of my courier to get the batteries from the farmhouse—or wherever they were charged—to and from the various sets.

With all the sets located, and marked on my map so that I could study where they were, we set out to return to Champgenéteux. The job had been done without incident, which we were both pleased about. René was relieved to be out of the villages we had had to visit, reiterating to me what I already knew—it was best to avoid villages. If a German got killed anywhere nearby, others would just go into the village and take people randomly off the streets as hostages. They would have them shot as retribution, driving home the message to everyone that the Germans were in charge and could do what they liked to the population.

It was sometime in mid-May when I got back to La Roisière, Paul's mother's abandoned old farm on the outskirts of Champgenéteux where Claude and René had set up shop not too long before I was parachuted in. I now prepared to meet the other members of Scientist.

TEN

CATCH ME IF YOU CAN

OVER THE NEXT DAY OR SO AT THE LITTLE ABANDONED farmhouse, Claude de Baissac (code name Denis) introduced me to the rest of the Scientist network. He was undoubtedly the leader who ran the show—nobody was in any doubt about that. René (Verger) was, of course, second-in-charge, but there were more network members to meet.

First was Claude's sister Lise de Baissac. Claude talked in glowing terms of her work with him in Bordeaux the previous year and what they had achieved together there. At thirty-nine, Lise (code name now Marguerite) was a lot older than me. Her training reports commented on her cool, calm, and collected manner, and I could see why.

While in England between missions, Lise had broken her leg while assisting with parachute training for two new female F Section agents, Yvonne Baseden and Violette Szabo, which had slowed her return to France. I did not know Violette at the time, but did know *of* her. Yvonne and I met after the war, and kept in touch. We were among the youngest women to join SOE.

Lise had arrived back in France in April 1944, this time by

Lysander, as parachuting was not ideal for a recently mended leg. She was destined for the Pimento network, but that did not go well. They were not politically aligned and did not get on, so Lise requested to be moved so she could work with her brother. I imagine that—with so many different factions on the ground to contend with—Baker Street could see the benefit of her ability to diffuse tensions, which would balance Claude's rather brash nature. Next, Claude introduced me to twenty-two-year-old Maurice Larcher (code name Vladimir). Like Claude and Lise (and my mother), Maurice came from Mauritius, where he had spent time in the Territorial Army. I think it must have been highly unusual to have four people with Mauritian heritage in a network of six, and I suspect that this was not random. Buckmaster must have thought it was a strength. Maurice was a tall, strong-looking young man who seemed quite reserved. Maurice's courier would be René and the two were to be based north of Caen, as would I. Claude, as he had already told me, would stay farther south and keep on the move. Maurice had already been in and around his area with René for some time, helping set things up.

As René was to be Maurice's courier, it meant that Lise or Katia would be mine.

"You will take Lise as your courier," came the short statement from Claude.

This was not what I wanted to hear. The impression I'd been given in London was that I would be able to choose my courier.

"I don't want to," was my bold reply. Not wanting him to think once more that a British colonial woman was telling him what to do, I quickly softened it.

"I think Katia and I would pair well, and that means you and Lise can work together again."

I was trying to sell this as a stroke to Claude's ego, given the successful work history of the de Baissac siblings. I was hoping he would see it as a unique opportunity to work together again and make a further impression on Baker Street in the closing months of the war. Well, he was not happy but he did eventually give me Katia.

I heard later that Claude had specifically recruited Katia to the Scientist network "for his pleasure." I am not sure whether any pleasure was had—Katia and I did not stay together all the time—but the comment did not surprise me as liaisons between agents were not uncommon. I also read in a book that Lise had said she couriered for me—but for the record, Lise de Baissac was never my courier, Katia was. There was another story about Lise going through a checkpoint with me while carrying a piece of my equipment. Apparently, it wasn't picked up when she was searched, but she then dropped it as she went through and the officer, unusually, took no notice. That may well have happened to her, but it did not happen with me.

* * *

I ALSO BRIEFLY MET Jean Séailles, a twenty-eight-year-old Parisian. Séailles was commissioned in July 1944 as a member of the British Army and therefore became a locally recruited SOE agent without ever coming to the UK during the war. Fifty-one other Frenchmen were locally recruited as SOE agents in World War II. Being French, Commandant Séailles worked with the FFI (French Forces of the Interior—we called them "Free from Infection" as a joke).

Séailles and his wife, Krino, had been busy organizing the Maquis of Saint-Mars-du-Désert in the Mayenne, which was our region.

Free France had ordered them to establish themselves in the Mayenne so that arms and explosives could be received on a large scale for use by guerrilla troops and saboteurs. Through Paul at the Navarre network, Séailles and Krino were now also using La Roisière in Champgenéteux as their base. Paul had connected them with Claude, who was also in touch with the FTP group in Saint-Mars-du-Désert.

Via Scientist, there were now links to London from the Resistance on the ground in the Mayenne. Claude said they would be working closely together to disperse the increasing number of arms and explosives being parachuted in, to multiple saboteurs, in preparation for the impending Allied invasion. I am sure that Claude's intention was, again, to build up a secret army that he would have sway over with the help of people like Séailles, who had gathered together some two thousand fifteen- and sixteen-year-olds who did not want to be sent off to forced labor camps. The two men were perfect for each other: Claude wanted the numbers, and Séailles wanted the arms.

Having said that, though, I don't think they really got along. It was more a marriage of convenience. There was something about Séailles that I didn't like, and likewise a man called Mickey, otherwise known as Edmond Duval, who seemed to be Séailles's second-in-command. I made a mental note to avoid them if at all possible.

I wanted to be well out of the politics of it all. Distributing equipment and armory and recruiting people on the ground to do the dirty work wasn't anything I needed or wanted to be involved in, and nor was doing any sabotage myself. It was my job to find information while moving from place to place, especially troop movements, and pass that back to home base. Of course, I would also send and receive messages about *parachutages* and any other information the network needed to communicate about. This information would come via the couriers. Katia and Lise would meet on their own "sked" every two days, to exchange intelligence. Then Maurice or I, as radio operators, would pass it along as needed, keeping the all-important link to London alive for Scientist.

With D-Day less than a month away, there was a huge amount of SOE and Resistance/Maquis activity across Normandy. Clearly some tensions were coming to a head between the English and the French on the ground, both trying to work for the same outcome of a liberated France—but with different masters. Early in the war, SOE had originally set up two sections in France: F Section (which usually worked independently from Charles de Gaulle and had non-French agents), and RF Section (working with de Gaulle and supporting the Maquis). The operations in France were essentially led from London, where communication with the British authorities provided the material needed to get to France so that the resisters on the ground could cause chaos for their German occupiers. If it was a delicate dance in England, it was even more so in France where the real work took place.

Dr. Paul Janvier would write in his 1970 memoir about a meeting on May 12, 1944, at his house with Claude, René, and Philippe Sergeant, a representative of General de Gaulle's BCRA—the Bureau Central de Renseignements et d'Action (the Central Bureau of Intelligence and Action). The meeting did not go well; Paul described it as "cold." Claude was unimpressed that Paul was in contact with representatives of de Gaulle, whom he felt should not have a say in the networks working to liberate France. Claude's attitude was worrying to Paul—after he and René left, Paul had to reassure the visiting envoy that he would not be influenced by SOE, who, as they knew, also seemed to have links with communist partisans. Paul assured Philippe that there was nothing to fear from the Resistance group he was running in the region and it would remain solely under the military orders of France.

"With my men and British equipment, I organized throughout our region so that, when the day came, we had an underground army ready to obey General de Gaulle's orders, setting aside any differences in political views," he wrote.

This tangled and somewhat dry information is only provided here to give some sense of the complex political passions that existed and the myriad factions swirling around on the ground. Politics always seems to complicate matters, and this is magnified in wartime. The war was bad enough in itself without trying to figure out who you could trust, even if they appeared to be on the same side as you. Looking back, I recall it was tiring. Although it sounds strange, I have always maintained that I could never trust the French. That's a broad statement to make—and of course I trusted *some* French people—but it was always difficult to fully ascertain what a person's motives were. A collaborator would be just as nice to me as a patriot. The easiest—perhaps the only—way for me to survive this war zone was to trust very, very few people, blend into the fabric of the society I was working in, and just stay out of the way of trouble as much as I could.

★ ★ ★

TROUBLE WOULD SOON FIND me, though; it was never far away. About a week later, in late May, a nearby farmer alerted the Gestapo to the location of the Mont du Saule site where I had landed three weeks before. It had proved to be a useful site for Paul and his wider Resistance team, and there had been other deliveries of packages and containers since my arrival. Word was that they had also found parachutes. Having the site compromised was one thing, but there were other consequences: finding a drop zone meant that the Gestapo would be on the hunt for both who and what had been dropped there. The circle of possibility from that one site was wide—they would be looking in a 360-degree direction and quite some distance away from the site itself.

The network quickly alerted us that the site had been found, and also that the Gestapo suspected there must be Englishmen in Champgénéteux. Someone had heard English being spoken there. When I heard that, my heart dropped. I knew I had not spoken English in the short time I had been there before leaving to find the sets. And I'd hardly been seen anyway, apart from a public meet-and-greet with my "grandparents." And I had certainly not spoken English in the few days I had been back in the area preparing to head away with Katia. Had a collaborator seen me, suspected that I was not the fourteen-year-old soap-selling granddaughter I purported to be, and called the Gestapo to hunt me down?

The Gestapo had already made inquiries at Bais, Paul's village, which was as good as on our doorstep. The friendly gendarmerie in Bais let us know that the Gestapo were on their way to Champgénéteux at two o'clock in the morning, so we left La Roisière in haste, burning documents before we did so—including my notes on where my seventeen sets were located. I had one brief last look at them, confident that I could re-create the notes in my head and knowing that my Michelin map would take me close enough to trigger the mental images that would take me to the exact place.

Under the cover of darkness and with help from others, Paul and Georges Baguenard rapidly moved all incriminating evidence and equipment that night to another location far from Champgenéteux. Although his doctor's car, complete with implicating cargo, was stopped by the local gendarmerie just down the road from his practice, they did not search it. A doctor traveling in the night would have good reason to do so, so should not be held up. The Bais gendarmerie was, in any case, friendly to the Resistance cause.

By the time the village of Champgenéteux was crawling with Gestapo, there was no evidence of anything or anyone suspicious to be found. Whether or not they found La Roisière on the outskirts and searched it, I do not know. Regardless, after this event it was considered off-limits for us.

Later, a grocer was found to be the collaborator who had told the Gestapo that he had overheard English. I heard that a plane had crashed, and some partisans were taking the surviving crew to the coast to try to get them back to England on a fishing boat across the Channel. Whether that was fact or fiction, I do not know. It was so hard to figure out what was true at the time. Every fishing boat had two Germans stationed on it, but there were stories circulating of fishing boats vanishing with their German passengers never being found. The type of English that was overheard, apparently, was American. It would not have been British. In a situation like that one, the British would do as they were told. No conversation— you just shut up and go with the partisans. But being Americans, I imagine they would question everything. The Americans certainly operated a little differently than the British.

With all our agents having fled the area to take refuge at various places some way away, Paul and the local Resistance network turned their attention to moving the accumulated weaponry from its current hiding place to somewhere safer. It was hidden in livestock fodder and transported at night. As expected, a few days later the Germans attacked everywhere in the region, searching for evidence of what must have been dropped. The work the Resistance did for the British was risky and hard, and the villages and the people in them paid the price. I am sure that the determination of the Resistance would have worn thin at times if there was friction with the English, as it seemed there continued to be between Paul and Claude.

Paul's memoir notes that after these events in May, "my relations were then quite difficult with Claude de Baissac who still claims to impose English authority on me. For me, I stand my ground, as do all the leaders of my groups whose attitudes reinforce my convictions."

* * *

LIFE ON THE ROAD for Katia and me meant living outdoors. We were never seen together during the day, but aimed to meet at the end of every other day at an agreed place on the map, somewhere secluded. On the other days I was on my own as she would be meeting Lise to exchange information. We slept in forests, which were abundant in Normandy. It was the cusp of summer, so thankfully we were not often cold. At night we would travel to stay close to the German army—when they moved, we moved, and when the sun was up, so were we. Our lives were ruled by the rise and fall of the sun. And curfews.

Food was scarce. During the day, we separately scavenged what we could on our travels and brought our mutual offerings together for our once-a-day meal at the end of it. I left the cooking to Katia. She carried a pot and something to sit it on, and would get a fire going with twigs and sticks we gathered. We would get water from a well at a local farm and then add our ingredients to said pot. The Germans who were billeted at the farms often ate peas, and the discarded pods would usually be in a cardboard box at the back of the house ready to go to the pigs. When getting the water, we would swipe a handful of them as the basis of our boil-up. Turnips were not too difficult to find, either, so they often went in. If we were lucky, we might find some mushrooms or wild onions to give it some flavor.

I thought I was destined to become a full-time vegetarian, but one night Katia announced that she had caught a squirrel. They were cheeky little things and Katia had managed to get close enough to one to deal to it with a piece of wood. She took the innards out and then smoked it fur and all, although the fur did burn off a bit. As an animal lover I felt sorry for the squirrel, but I have to say it tasted good. A few weeks later, skinnier than we had been as we were steadily losing weight—by the time I left France, I would only weigh seventy-four pounds—we visited a farmhouse where Katia knew the people in the Resistance there. It was a safe option for us. They asked if we would like to eat with them and it was an instant yes: the smell of cooking was lovely.

"Have you eaten squirrel before?" inquired the woman.

"Oh yes," we both said, having eaten a few by then. We tucked into the squirrel stew, grateful for the hot meal and their compassion in sharing with us what meager food they had themselves.

As we left later that evening, they told us that it was actually rat stew but they had thought they shouldn't tell us before we ate it. It turns out that rat tastes okay.

Finding the sets without the notes did prove to be no trouble—my excellent memory served me correctly. We also navigated checkpoints with no concerns. The authenticity of my papers was never doubted, I could answer any questions about what I was doing, and the Morse key I had hidden up inside the springs under my bike seat was never discovered. So far, so good.

The Resistance workers on the ground created an arms depot in the Forêt de Pail, to the northeast of Bais, and located a new airdrop site nearby. Its location was passed on to London so that the drops could continue. The messages I sent were quick, to avoid detection by the dreaded German direction-finders. If they picked up any activity, they would use triangulation to narrow the transmissions down to a certain area. To get it narrowed down further would entail an on-foot search by the Gestapo. This was why we had to transmit from multiple, changing places and keep messages short—you needed to transmit and then shut down quickly, hide the set and leave the area. Your location could be traced within about twenty minutes, and everyone in the area would then be searched. You did not want to be there when they went looking.

The environment I was cycling through showed the awful ravages of war. While some eighty days of fighting were yet to come between D-Day and the liberation of Paris, this period before D-Day had already seen a lot of damage done to the people and the landscape of Normandy. From the start of 1944, the aerial bombardment from the Allies on the northern coasts of France and Belgium was aimed at disrupting communication lines, damaging the transport infrastructure, and weakening the German positions in preparation for the D-Day landings. The Allies carried out identical bombardment missions in Germany as well, so as not to arouse suspicion about Normandy being the chosen location for an invasion.

While the targeted bombing of strategic road and rail junctions would make it difficult for Germany to get reinforcements to the front line, a lot of those road and rail targets were in French villages and cities. Bombing was not always a precise art, either, and the powers that be felt that any lack of quality could be helped by increasing the quantity. Collateral damage also occurred due to Allied pilots dealing with clouds and flying at high altitudes to avoid antiaircraft fire from the ground. Bombs could not be left in the aircraft as that would make landing back in England dangerous. Although "spare" bombs were often used for secondary sites, some were dropped in areas as deserted as possible, but still, sadly, would hit civilian homes.

In April 1944, even British prime minister Winston Churchill expressed his concern at the collateral damage caused by bombing raids along the northern coast of France in preparation for Operation Overlord (the name for the D-Day military operation). But this was war. From the air they could not see what I could see on the ground—which was ugly. The people of Normandy were paying a huge price for the liberty that they so greatly wanted. My presence in the area would also add to their woes.

* * *

THIS BECAME EVIDENT ONE time when I returned to my pseudo-grandparents' home to gather soap to sell in Champgenéteux. Monsieur Durand warned me that the Gestapo had recently searched their farmhouse a couple of times. The Germans obviously knew that there was new radio activity in the area and were on the hunt for the culprit.

On this particular day, I had sent a message while the German officer who was billeted with my "grandparents" was out. About half an hour later, having hidden the set away, I was in the old, ruined stables out the back looking for the best place to hide some extra parts I had just ordered for my radio sets, which would be coming on the next drop. Suddenly I could hear Monsieur Durand start to talk quite loudly with someone, so I went back into the house to see what was going on. And there, standing at the front door, were some Gestapo officers.

I did not avoid them, but rather went straight up to join my "grand-père," unconcerned. I could hear the men asking him whether anyone had come by wanting eggs from the geese he had on the farm, and where Madame Durand was. She was out shopping.

Monsieur Durand immediately introduced me as his grand-daughter from Paris. "I know," came the quick reply from one of the officers. That told me that our public greeting orchestrated by Paul had been noticed and passed on. One of the Gestapo was a man, the other a woman, and both were very nice—overly nice, in fact, as they kept up with their questions.

"Did you enjoy the trip? When did you arrive?"

Well, my story was all down pat, so I had no problem answering those questions. I was very friendly, very accommodating—almost excited, like a naive fourteen-year-old might be about a new life. When they asked for my papers, I happily handed them over. They were examined in silence, handed back, and then came the step forward into the house to start the search. No asking, just marching in.

Farmhouses then didn't have toilets, only commodes. The one in this house was in the passageway between the bedrooms. Back then they were roughly made, quite solid, and—as I'd recently discovered—were handily constructed to just the right proportions to make a perfect hiding place. I had found I could break up the set and fit pieces of it under the seat of the commode. It was a snug fit and nothing moved. It was also very hard to see.

The two officers stopped in the hallway right beside the commode. I made a point of always keeping the chamber pot half-full so that it was obvious it was in use. This did not seem to deter their interest in it.

"Remove!" came the direction, pointing at the pot. I duly did so and walked out the back door with it to throw the contents away, then used the water pump outside to rinse it out. On my return I could see them examining the structure, looking for hinges or the like that would signal a secret compartment. To my great (but hidden) relief, they seemed satisfied that there was nothing suspicious and set to searching the rest of the house.

Looking back, I wonder if they were looking for a woman—was this the reason they had come to search the house for the third time in as many weeks and were suspicious of me? I learned after the war that, to experts, the way I sent a message would have looked different from a man's message. Women often sent at a faster speed. I was also using the new Morse key that was different from the keys others would be using with those sets, so I wasn't using my wrist as you would with the standard key. These nuances would have been obvious to experts listening to transmissions.

When the Gestapo pair came back to the front door, "grandpère" and I were just outside busying ourselves with getting me ready to head off on my bike. He was packing soap balls into the basket on the front of the bike, while I was asking him about the route he thought I should take. "Grandpère" turned to our visitors and asked them what they might suggest. Clever, really, as this normalized my task. "Grandpère" explained that their billeted officer would usually give me directions on where the army was so I could head straight to them with my soap. There was a bit of discussion between the Gestapo officers before they gave some instructions to my "grandpère." He followed it up with, "And how many checkpoints does she go through?" Two was the answer.

The pair seemed satisfied that all was well in the Durand house, and turned to leave. As they did so, the man pulled out his revolver and I could see Monsieur Durand's face fall. He sighed and looked down at his feet. The gun was pointed up at the ceiling, three shots were fired, and they promptly left.

I was relieved, but "grandpère" was angry. Not only was this the third visit in three weeks, but also the third set of holes in the ceiling.

★ ★ ★

A SHORT TIME LATER there was yet another visit from another lot of Gestapo. This time I answered the door and turned on my fourteen-year-old charm. I answered their questions like an excited kid and wouldn't stop talking. I showed them my soap, and my map of where I thought I might sell it. They didn't stay long. Perhaps they realized that their comrades had just visited. Or perhaps they got sick of me being annoying.

Now that I had told two groups of Gestapo that I was going, I had to follow through. As soon as these ones left I set off on my bike, waving cheerily to "grandpère." I did not feel so happy inwardly—this had been a close call. I later found out that the Gestapo had arrested people in the village and I felt responsible. They had done nothing wrong—they had simply been arrested to remind the villagers that anyone could be detained on the slightest suspicion of Resistance behavior.

One night soon after that—a night I was on my own, without Katia—I located a set just outside the local village, in some bombed-out stables. I needed to meet my sked and report on the position of the German troops I had successfully sold soap to that day, along with some other snippets of conversation I had overheard. The stables were away from the farmhouse down a secluded pathway—the hiding place had come back to me clearly as soon as I saw the path.

Mostly roofless, but there was still enough of the building left to keep it half-standing. A bit of wall or two, and even part of a window on one side. I assembled the set on a bit of firm rubble and achieved what I needed to do in quick order. I was just about to hide the various pieces of the set again among the ruins when I heard a noise outside. I could see two German soldiers coming down the path toward me—thankfully from the end of the building that was still semistanding. I quickly turned the set around with the lid standing up so they could not see what was inside.

It was soon obvious from their stumbles that they had had too much cider. I was wondering how they had managed to get to the stables. Had they gotten lost on the way back to where they were meant to be? Were they hungry and hoping to steal some eggs from the geese they thought might be there? Or—had they followed me? Whatever it was, they must surely be wondering what I was doing there.

As the pair reached the stables and saw me, I acted like I was in a panic—not at them discovering me, though. "Don't come close," I shouted, waving them away and making to cover my mouth. "I'm not well—I think I've got scarlet fever."

In the early twentieth century, scarlet fever was a leading cause of death in children. Even now it was still something to be feared without access to antibiotics, and I was banking on them knowing that. Penicillin was the drug needed to treat the sore throat and fever that came with the disease, and it was currently being mass-produced for treating infections in wounded soldiers. The remote possibility of a girl like me in small-town France getting access to penicillin was hopefully appropriate to the panic I was displaying.

It occurred to me that the men might recognize me from selling soap earlier in the day.

"I've sold all my soap, and I'm going home now. I'm too sick to keep going," I added as I closed the case. This particular set was in a perfectly normal-looking little suitcase—they had no reason to believe there was anything in there but my own things. I also hoped that they thought that the soap was stored in the stables and that was why I was out there.

My mind was racing. I was not panicking, but I was certainly scared. It would be truthful to say that I was scared the whole time I was in France—just more scared at some times than others. This was one of those times.

Although I had my story about Champgenéteux and my "grandparents" ready, it was not necessary. The men were young and on their own, and I concluded that, with a skinful of cider, they'd been thinking they were going to have a bit of fun with a young girl. Added to the risk of being a secret agent was also that of being female. But this time that also worked in my favor—they were fixated on me being young and female, not thinking of anything more dangerous like the suspicious behavior of a secret agent.

Thankfully, they must have decided it was not worth the risk that I would make them sick. They turned around and stumbled back up the path.

ELEVEN

CAUGHT AND QUESTIONED BY THE GESTAPO

THE NEXT TIME KATIA AND I MET UP, WE WOKE IN A secluded wooded area quite some miles from the coast, just as the sun rose. I did not have a watch, so, as always, my day was ruled by the rise and fall of the sun along with the odd church bell to give me clues as to the time of day. It was a warm, summery day and we had our usual hug goodbye after planning to meet some nineteen miles away, farther along the coast in the direction of Saint-Lô. That distance was an average sort of day on the bike, but we both thought we might make slower progress given the increased number of German soldiers we had encountered in this area in the preceding days. Like us, they knew something was brewing with the Allies.

Because of the situation, we also decided on a plan B meeting point not quite as far away, and near to another of my seventeen hidden sets. Anything that either of us observed during the day could then be fed into my messages back to London later that night.

As was our usual practice, Katia set off ahead of me so that we weren't seen together. If for some reason we needed a connection to each other, we had decided to pretend that she was my auntie. After Katia left, I patted myself down to remove any foliage picked up from the forest floor and ran my hands through my hair to check for plant matter and to smooth it down. I did not want anyone to suspect I had been sleeping out in the open. In the early-morning light I did a final check to make sure my soap was in the saddlebag, along with my knitting—the staple items I always needed with me on my bike to align with my alias and allow me to contact England. And of course my Morse key was secured under the bike seat. All was in order, so I headed off toward the coast. The imposing and newly strengthened Atlantic Wall meant that I could not get right to the coast itself, but as Normandy was pretty flat I could see it from time to time if I was on a road that was slightly elevated like the one I was traveling on that day.

Stopping on the rise of a small hill, I allowed myself the luxury of observing the morning routine for the local fishermen I could make out in the distance. I watched them, clad in weather-worn clothing and rubber boots, carefully pushing their boats into the water at what was obviously deemed to be a safe place by the German officers who always went with them. Some of the boats looked to be powered by small engines; others seemed to be reliant on oars and sails. They must have been hardy men, used to the strong tides and rough waters of northern France, and expert at timing their run for the best chance of catching fish. With food being scarce, their hard work kept their families fed—if, of course, their German crews allowed them to keep some of the catch, which was primarily destined for their troops. Life under occupation was hard for the

Normans, and I hoped that the rumors of the Allied invasion not being far away was providing them some much-needed hope.

Although watching the fishermen made me feel hungry, I had become accustomed to ignoring the gnawing feeling in my stomach. With luck I would be able to find some food somewhere along the way. I hoped it would be more than just turnips, which had become my standard fare, but any food would be acceptable. Raw turnips were not enjoyable, but they were still food. I could not afford to be fussy. Water, though, was essential—and had the useful advantage of filling me up—so I always kept an eye out for pumps at the back of farmhouse sheds. If I ran into the farmer, they were usually alright about me taking some water, but often there was nobody about.

Turning away, I biked on through the Normandy countryside. The roads in this region, especially those leading to the coast, were often narrow and winding. They were lined with tall hedgerows and flanked by deep ditches, which made them challenging to navigate for military vehicles but easy enough for me on my bike, if a little bumpy. The challenges of the natural landscape had already been communicated to England by previous operatives, and would have been taken into consideration when planning the upcoming D-Day landings. Those hedgerows were going to present quite a challenge for the invading Allied forces, as they would provide cover for German defenders. Besides that, some roads were so narrow that larger military vehicles would find them difficult.

The warmer weather meant that blossoms were adorning the orchards I passed, their delicate petals carrying the scent of spring on the wind. If this had not been wartime, I could perhaps have better appreciated the spring scenery. To me, though, the blossoms were simply the promise of fruit on trees as an easy food source later.

Farther along the coast, on another slightly hilly bit of terrain, I could see that other fishermen had already come ashore and their German guards were heading off (complete with the catch). I wondered if any of them might make a break for England if they could deal with their German minders on board, as I had heard might have happened a few times.

I had only been through this particular area a couple of times since finding all my sets with René when I first arrived, so I was not overly familiar with the roads. I could see on my Michelin map that there was another town just beyond the long stretch of straight road I was on. I reminded myself that road signs, if they were even still there and not painted over, were not to be trusted given German or collaborator interference. With a corner coming up ahead in the distance, too, I suspected there might be a checkpoint. These were always around a corner, and I felt overdue for one today.

I slowed down, looking for a secret sign from Katia that she had also come this way and warned me about an upcoming checkpoint. Her signals to me were different every time, using the natural elements on offer so as not to arouse the suspicions of the German army. I knew to look for the unusual. Beside a group of shrubs, I got off my bike as if to check something on it. The middle shrub was a spiky sort of plant, and on closer inspection I could see that a couple of leaves from the plant beside it had been picked and threaded onto the thorny parts of this middle shrub. That was my sign: there was indeed going to be a checkpoint around the corner.

They were set up around a corner for a reason. A soldier with a machine gun was always positioned as soon as you came around the corner—if you turned around upon seeing them, that was highly

In March 1944, just weeks before parachuting into Normandy, Pippa walks the streets of London.

(Pippa Latour private collection)

The Crance crew who dropped Pippa into Normandy on May 2, 1944.

(Ray McCall)

Colonel Maurice Buckmaster, the leader of the French (F) section of SOE in Pippa's time, pictured at home in England in 1957. *(Popperfoto/Getty Images)*

Claude de Baissac, who ran the Scientist circuit (Resistance network). *(Wikimedia Commons/UK Government circa 1945)*

Madame and Monsieur Durand outside their farmhouse in Champgenéteux. The couple posed as Pippa's grandparents when she took on the identity of Paulette.

(Pippa Latour private collection)

RIGHT: A portrait of Pippa in late 1944, after her return from France.

(Pippa Latour private collection)

Pippa (right) with her dear friend Barbara Cox.
(Pippa Latour private collection)

BELOW: A copy of a telegram that Pippa penned for Barbara during the war. It is unclear whether the message was ever sent. The text reads: "Darling Barbie, I have a little time for this scribbled note. Keep your chin up little soldier & till we next meet. Thanks darling for helping me through all these years, I will try & make you proud of me. Tons & tons of love, Pippa."
(Pippa Latour private collection)

POST OFFICE

INLAND
TELEGRAM

FOR POSTAGE STAMPS

For conditions of acceptance, see over.

Chargeable Words	Counter Number
Charge	

....M.

Prefix	Handed in	SERVICE INSTRUCTIONS	Actual Words	To.....................................

If you wish to pay for a reply insert **R.P.** here

ADDRESS (Preferably in BLOCK letters).

Darling Barbie, I have a little time for this scribbled note. Keep your chin up little soldier, & till we next meet. Thanks darling for helping me through all these years, I will try & make you proud of me. Tons & tons of love Pippa

The name and address of the sender, and telephone number (if any) should be written on the back of this form.

Pippa in Auckland, circa 1960s, with her four children. From left: Odette, Pauline, Pippa, Brendon, and Barry. *(Pippa Latour private collection)*

Laurent Contini, the French ambassador to New Zealand, speaks to Pippa prior to presenting her with the Chevalier de l'Ordre National de la Légion d'Honneur, France's highest military decoration, in November 2014. *(Michael Bradley/AFP via Getty Images)*

Pippa celebrates Christmas 2020 at home with her friend Peter Wheeler, the former CEO of the New Zealand Bomber Command Association Inc. *(Peter Wheeler collection)*

RIGHT: Pippa and her longtime friend Lyn Macdonald in March 2023, a couple of weeks before Pippa's 102nd birthday. *(Lyn Macdonald collection)*

Even though that seat had been looked at in previous checkpoints, I breathed a silent sigh of relief when he moved on without finding my Morse key in the springs.

He turned his attention back to me and continued to study my face intently. For a moment, it felt as if time was standing still. Another question came. "Have you always been living there?"

I had not been asked for this level of detail before, but I knew exactly what to say: "When my school closed in Paris I could not get back to my home in the Belgian Congo, so I was kept in France and sent up here to my grandparents to help look after them."

The officer mused on that for a moment, staring away from me into the distance. Then, with an almost imperceptible nod, he handed me back my identification card and looked me straight in the eye. I was fully expecting the order to move on through the checkpoint. Instead, he waved his hand in the direction of the gatehouse, meaning that I should join the group of half a dozen or so people already there with their bikes. Turning away, he moved his gaze to the person behind me as if I was no longer of any consequence.

I wheeled my bike to the gatehouse and was about to park it and join the group of people standing there when they were suddenly moved off under the guidance of a soldier who had just come out of the guardhouse. I was motioned to join them, so parked my bike and caught them up on foot. We were led to the truck on the other side of the checkpoint; as I got closer, I could see that the back was open and there were already some twenty people sitting inside. We were herded in like animals being put into a cattle truck. I was one of the last to enter. Walking down the central part of the truck to the last available space to sit, I carefully avoided stepping on anyone's feet facing inward into the aisle. Having sat, I looked around and surveyed my fellow travelers. There were men and women of all ages—and Katia was there. She had not gotten through the checkpoint after all. We showed no sign of knowing each other.

✦ ✦ ✦

IT WAS A SHORT ride to the town police station, about ten minutes. Here we were herded off the truck again and divided into two groups. The men were led off through one door and we women through another. I counted thirteen of us. Thirteen unlucky women. I found my thoughts wandering to my bike and worrying whether anyone would steal my soap. I would soon, however, have more serious things to worry about.

We were put into a waiting room sort of area with lots of chairs. The German officer who had shown us in suggested we take a seat, saying that someone would be back with us shortly. He shut the door and left. We all sat in silence, wondering what was to happen next.

When the door opened again, it was a woman in the gray-green uniform of the Gestapo who entered. It was unusual to see a female Gestapo officer. She had an imposing manner, and carried herself with the typical Gestapo haughtiness that showed she knew she held all the power. However, when she spoke, it belied her appearance. She appeared to be reassuring, with—perhaps purposely—softened words in French.

"Ladies. Please don't be nervous, there is no need. Yes, we are in a police station, and you might think you are under arrest, but really, we are just doing some standard checks in this area today and we hopefully won't hold you up for long. I am sure you have nothing to hide."

Then the instruction came: "What I will need you to do is to undress here." She then pointed to a curtained area at the back of the room. "And I will call you individually to come and see me there."

Before walking to the back of the room she looked directly at Katia, who was at the front, and said, "Let's start with you, shall we." It was a statement, not a question. And as she passed me at the back of the room, she gave a thin smile and added, "And you can be next."

The curtains opened, then closed behind her. The group of women began removing their clothes. I had deliberately not stood anywhere near Katia, so it seemed odd that we had been singled out to go in first and second. Did they suspect we knew each other? My logical mind knew that this was highly unlikely, but I still felt a flicker of concern. However, I put any unease to one side—my training had made me aware that the enemy would want to keep us guessing, would want us to wonder why things were the way they were, would want us to worry. The Gestapo officer's reassuring manner was also meant to disarm us, as if she was on our side and if we worked together there would be no problem.

We were all shapes, sizes, and ages. There was a mother with a daughter of about eight or nine, through to an older woman who might have been in her seventies. We remained silent apart from the mother talking quietly to her daughter—no doubt trying to explain the situation and ask her to comply quietly and not create any fuss. Being naked in a group of people was meant to dehumanize us, but I felt a quiet, proud defiance within our group.

I caught Katia's eye as she went in, with her clothes folded in her hands, and hoped that my deliberately calm face would make her feel calm too. She had nothing on her that would be incriminating. It was I who had something hidden—the silk codes inside my hair

171

ribbon-cum-shoelace, and we both knew it was all over for me if they were found.

Of course the curtain did not screen sound, only vision. I heard Katia being asked the usual questions about her identity and where she was heading. Katia spoke when she was spoken to and offered nothing more. There was obviously some sort of physical examination, and then the all clear was given and she came out clutching her clothes and papers and started getting dressed. She shot a clandestine look at me. I could tell she was worried that I would be found out because of my hair tie.

When I was called in, I was invited to sit down in front of the desk the Gestapo woman was sitting behind, and asked to put my clothes on the desk and my shoes on the floor in front of me. There was another woman standing behind her. The Gestapo officer smiled as she examined my papers, and continued to smile at me as she checked my photo against my face. In fact, I would describe her face as dripping honey—but I knew exactly what she was really doing. She was anything but sweet.

I answered the usual questions about my identity exactly as I had done at the checkpoint. I met her falsely warm tone not in the same manner, but like a fourteen-year-old with nothing to hide would. I did not offer more than I needed to, but I wasn't frosty either. I didn't want to inflame the situation. The Gestapo officer seemed satisfied that my paperwork was in order, and that I was who I said I was. The other woman in the room then went through my clothes and shoes. There was nothing there of interest—just a faded old blue cotton dress and peasanty-looking footwear.

We moved to the last part of the interrogation. Again, our conversation was all in French.

"Paulette, stand up while we examine you," came the instruction. The other woman snapped a pair of thin rubber gloves on, signaled that I should put my arms out, and patted my body down, lifting my arms to look in my armpits, and asking me to show the undersides of my feet. She looked in my ears, up my nose, and in my mouth. Then: "Let your hair out."

This was the real test. If they examined my hair tie closely they would find my codes inside it. I reached up to my ponytail and carefully felt for the knot to undo. Given the lack of money around, there would not have been anything suspicious in using a flat shoe-lace to tie my hair. A pretty ribbon would have been unheard of. I had of course made it my own—as a fourteen-year-old might do—by adding those woolen pompoms at each end.

My long hair fell over my shoulders as I held the potentially in-criminating hair tie in my hand. The woman moved behind me and felt my head with both hands, then asked me to put my head upside down and shake it vigorously. When I was allowed to stand back up, she then ran her hands roughly through my hair. I was wait-ing for the request to see my hair tie, but thankfully it didn't come and, inside my head, I breathed a huge, silent sigh of relief. Instead, there was a final instruction: "Now bend over." It felt intrusive and unnecessary, but I knew it was coming. I had been warned in my training about strip searches and what they entailed.

When she had finished, the woman came around to the front and looked me up and down like some sort of specimen she was exam-ining. Please, please don't ask to look at the hair tie, I willed her in my head. After what seemed like an eternity, the Gestapo woman issued a terse farewell: "Finish, finish. Go now." The warmth in her voice had evaporated completely.

I quickly gathered my clothes, shoes, and papers and left. Back in the big space I put my clothes back on and was then ushered back outside to the truck. There were already a few men in there, and Katia of course. When she looked up and saw it was me, I could see the relief on her face. I moved to the back, sat opposite her, and together we waited for thirty minutes or so while the rest of the truck filled up. When the last woman climbed in, it made thirteen of us—the same number that had arrived on the truck. I am not sure whether all the men were released, but the truck seemed full enough when the engine started and we pulled away from the police station.

A few minutes later we were back at the checkpoint, but before we could leave we all had to tell the soldiers what our destination was and what time we thought we would be there. This was a regular question, designed to make you think they were monitoring your every move—they would call ahead to the destination, saying to expect you. If you didn't turn up, then that was suspicious. They would go looking for you or flag you as a potential problem for the next time you went through a checkpoint. Whether or not the German army had the capacity to do all those things we never knew, which of course was all part of their control plan.

Katia picked up her bike and went through before me, mentioning our closer option B destination when asked. I overheard her answer as I was walking back to my bike, so gave the same destination. Before getting on my bike, I checked the saddlebags to see if the soap was still there, and was somewhat surprised to find that it was. It brought a smile to my face to think it had not been stolen by the soldiers at the checkpoint. I did not dare to check whether the Morse key was still under the seat. If it wasn't, of course, I would not be leaving the checkpoint.

Thankfully, I was waved through with just a cursory look at my papers. I pedaled away at a sensible pace—not too fast, or I could have looked like I was panicked. As I got around the corner without being called back by the soldier at the checkpoint, I breathed a sigh of relief—a real one this time.

As I rode on, I couldn't help but think about the dangerous game I was playing. This encounter with the Gestapo had been a close call. It was a reminder of the constant peril I faced as an undercover agent. I had much to put in my report to London later that evening.

TWELVE

D-DAY

KATIA AND I CONTINUED OUR GOOD WORK AS A TEAM and kept traveling, mostly without incident. She was an organized courier, ensuring that the batteries were kept charged, sometimes using the farms to do this while the billeted German officer was out. Officers would usually sleep in a bedroom inside the house, while a man of lesser rank would have a camp stretcher in the stables, so using these properties was always about the timing. Sometimes there would be a pedal type of generator available to charge the batteries, but it was complicated and the charge never seemed to stick very well. Traffic with London was busy. There was always information to share on my skeds, either from my own observances or information from the couriers. After I had transmitted my identification, they would say "message to follow, incoming," and I would jot down what they sent, hoping it was not too long. I would then send my own information to them. I liked to keep my messages to under 140 characters, so I could be all finished in thirty minutes. I pin-pricked the starting code I'd used on my piece of silk. Later, once I had used several codes, I would cut off the strip that had been

177

used and burn it. Once my work was done, I would shut down and get out of there as quickly as I could.

Being DF'ed (found by direction-finding equipment) was a constant concern. Once the DF people knew that something was being transmitted from within an area, they would let the Gestapo know and you could be found quickly. They would roam around in vehicles to narrow down where the signal was coming from. Sometimes they would even be on foot looking for you.

There was one occasion where I felt that I was in imminent danger of being found and needed help. At a location where I had seen some tanks, I was gathering information for my next sked as I sold soap to the German soldiers—and my heart sank when I spied a certain DF van nearby. It had several people in it—a man, a woman, a child, and a baby. I had seen this very same van a couple of days earlier, just after I had reported some German troop positions during my sked. Thankfully, they hadn't been able to locate me in time and I moved on immediately, cycling quite some distance away. The next day, the bombers had come in and hit the position I'd reported.

Now, I was again selling a death sentence along with my soap. But had they seen me? And had they seen me at the first place? I had certainly seen them. If they had indeed seen me, they would put two and two together: "She was there, it got bombed. She is here, it will now be bombed, therefore that soap-selling girl is a radio operator." They were not stupid. Straightaway, I used the courier system—Katia got in touch with Lise on her next sked, and Lise passed my message to Claude: "Take them out." And it was done.

When Katia and I reconnected a couple of days later, she told me that a grenade had been thrown at the DF van. All four people had been killed. I knew when reporting the van that it would be likely that the woman and the children I'd seen would die. It would have been too hard to just deal with the German direction-finder, the man who had been driving. I didn't know whether the woman was a collaborator or some poor thing who had been kidnapped randomly with her children to make the DF van look more authentic. I hoped it was not the latter, but it probably was. The van was of the type used by the local people—delivery vans, laundry vans, and the like—with the (German) driver in civilian clothes driving it farm to farm, village to village. Carrying a woman and children in the van would make him look even less suspicious. I wondered how the patriots who threw the grenade felt, and if they knew whether the passengers were collaborators or hostages. I guessed you threw it regardless.

Throwing grenades was something even the most ladylike of Resistance women were good at doing. When I next saw Simone, at Paul's home one night, she told me that she had acted on some information recently. Paul added that she had a good arm on her.

★ ★ ★

WHILE I WAS BACK in the area, albeit briefly, Paul organized for me to train some members of the local reception committee in the use of the Eureka beacon, so that they could guide aircraft in. I could sense that everyone was getting ready for the Allies to set foot on the Continent soon. If life was hard now, it was only going to get harder. I couldn't see the Germans rolling over in a hurry.

Claude visited to inform me we had a task in Paris at short notice. "A radio operator's set has been found—someone's betrayed us," he told me.

As there was no SOE agent close by, Claude needed me to get on a train to Paris with him. The radio operator was wounded, as were others, and we had to get them out. I needed to communicate with London about plans for a Lysander to pick them up.

Spending time with Claude was a chance for me to start getting along better with him, given the prickliness of some of our previous interactions. The most recent of these had also involved a train trip to Paris, this time without my knowledge. A radio set had been dropped at the same time as I was, but one of the valves had broken. While René and I were away on my familiarization trip, Claude had sourced a new valve and sent Katia off to Paris with the newly functioning set, to replace one that could not be found after a radio operator there had been killed (it certainly was a risky profession). Claude had decided to send the set there in the hope that another radio operator could soon be found.

When René and I returned, I was really annoyed at Claude for making that decision without consulting me and I let him know how I felt: "You know I wanted that set for Maurice [Vladimir]. It is my set to do with as I please, and you should not have sent it off."

It was a case of déjà vu. The colonial stuff reared its ugly head all over again and I saw a familiar expression come over his face. Once again, here was a British woman telling him what to do. For me, of course, it was not ethnicity—it was simply that he should not have made that decision without consulting me.

"Well, you have three sets," countered Claude, "and you don't need another."

It suddenly dawned on me that perhaps London hadn't told Claude that I had a lot more than the three sets hidden with my "grandparents" and the other two farmers. If Baker Street hadn't taken him into their confidence, I wondered, what did that mean? Anyway, the set was gone, and that was that. There were bigger things to think about, so I put it out of my mind.

Claude told me that the people who needed to be evacuated to England were under the care of La Coupole, a known safe house. Hearing that name—that favorite old haunt I'd gone to as a teenager with Grandfather—gave me a warm feeling inside. Of course, when we got there, the Paris I knew from that time was nothing like the Paris of 1944. Mind you, I was nothing like the carefree 1930s teenager I'd been, either.

I had assumed that Ivan was still at La Coupole because the location of the set I was to use was his home address. It did not surprise me that Ivan was in the Resistance. Of course he was. He was not at his house when I was doing my work, and nor did I expect him to be. I did what I needed to, and communicated the necessary arrangements to ensure we could get the wounded out. The word was that La Coupole was crawling with Germans, who suspected that it was a safe house. There would be no trip down memory lane for me. However, before we left the next day to travel north again, I got a message to go to a nearby park. It was there that I briefly saw Ivan, who had been told I was in town. Five years had passed since we had last seen each other, and the sight of his familiar, kind face made me feel emotional. It was likely that he was being watched closely, so we were both brief and cautious in our interaction.

Ivan let me know that Katia had been recruited by Lise at La Coupole. I was thankful she had, and told him I thought we were a good team.

"I always knew you would be the best little soldier." He smiled, as we parted ways. I did not know when I would see him again;

hopefully when life in Paris was back to something that we would both recognize.

I caught the train back with Claude, and never left Normandy or the Calvados area after that. D-Day was on the horizon, and that changed things for all of us.

* * *

IN PREPARATION FOR THE landings, the brief to SOE was to destroy all lines of German communication, to prevent enemy troops reaching the landing beaches, and to blow up railways, telephone lines, and fuel depots. In early June, Katia and I headed in one direction, Maurice and René in another, with Claude and Lise going somewhere else again. We all knew that D-Day, the invasion of Normandy, would be a pivotal turning point in the war, marking—if successful—the beginning of the end of Nazi Germany's control of Western Europe. The plan, code-named Operation Overlord, would be the largest seaborne invasion in history, and would involve a diverse coalition of American, British, Canadian, and other Allied troops.

Shortly before the D-Day landings, Radio Londres broadcast the opening lines of the poem "Chanson d'automne" by Paul Verlaine— *Les sanglots longs des violons de l'automne . . .* ("The long sobs of the violins of autumn . . .")—to let the Resistance know that the invasion was close. The lines that followed, on a later broadcast—*blessent mon cœur d'une langueur monotone* ("wound my heart with a monotonous languor")—signaled that Operation Overlord would start within forty-eight hours and the Resistance should begin sabotage operations, especially on the French railroad system. At this time,

Katia and I were making our way to Saint-Lô (about twenty-five miles from the coast), and learned of the imminent invasion from certain trusted people who had radios.

When it happened, it was something to behold, even some distance back from the coast.

"Katia—look," I said, glancing upward. Having been a balloon operator, I could recognize the objects shining in the sky in the morning light as balloons and knew the invasion was on. Nearly 160,000 Allied troops would land on the Normandy beaches early on the morning of June 6, 1944. It was not just an amphibious landing; there were also squadrons of aircraft bombing anything that moved, and others dropping paratroopers behind enemy lines. Some 11,000 Allied aircraft, 7,000 ships and boats, and thousands of other vehicles were involved in the invasion.

Everything went blank for the radio operators that day. You couldn't send anything. Chaos is how I would describe it. There was so much going on that you could not carry on as normal. Katia and I were at a checkpoint north of Saint-Lô when things started to heat up. Like us, the soldiers at the checkpoint were clearly wondering what would happen next. That question was answered by a big bang as one of the buildings near us was hit. Everyone scattered.

We decided it was best to go south to Vire, because in our minds we were going home. "It's happened, they won't need us now," I naively said to Katia. "We'll meet René and Maurice in Vire and see how we get out."

When we eventually got to Vire, it was obvious that the war was not just suddenly going to be over with the invasion. Now there was fighting, and lots of it. I stated the obvious to Katia: "We are not going home." We were still going to be needed—and now the situation was even more precarious, more dangerous, more desperate. How silly I was to have thought that the war would be over in a few days. Wishful thinking. SOE was still actively sending people in. On June 8, two days after the invasion, Violette Szabo parachuted in for a second time to play her part in keeping the advancing 2nd SS Panzer Division Das Reich from reaching the Normandy beaches. The SOE networks farther south of us did a magnificent job of slowing the enemy's journey time from Montauban to Normandy. The expected time to get there of three days turned into seventeen days—a significant delay that helped the Allies establish a bridgehead in Normandy. Sadly for brave Violette, who had volunteered for this second mission, her freedom would only last two days. She was arrested on June 10 by the advancing SS Panzer Division.

We got on our bikes again. As we headed back north, we came across a fisherman who described the carnage left behind from the invasion. Many of the bodies left floating in the water and on the beaches were now bloated, and the birds were using them as perches. As Katia and I got closer to the coast, we ourselves saw people staring at the ruins of their homes, dead horses—still attached to their carts—lying where they had fallen on the roads, and bombed villages. Historians would later estimate that a total of 4,414 Allied troops were killed on D-Day itself and more than 5,000 were wounded. In the Battle of Normandy that was to follow over the next three months, 73,000 Allied soldiers would be killed and 153,000 wounded. The same battle, along with Allied bombings of French villages and cities, would kill around 20,000 French civilians. The exact German casualties aren't known, but historians estimate that 4,000 to 9,000 men were killed, wounded, or missing during the D-Day invasion. There are some 22,000 German soldiers buried around Normandy.

Each time a transport truck passed us, we would stand aside while it went through at pace. The Americans were in a hurry to get to Paris. They did leave some handy things behind, though. We each managed to acquire a US Army–issue poncho, and it felt like a touch of luxury to have something between me and the forest floor and something on top as well.

Katia and I thought we should try to connect with Claude, to regroup, and spent a couple of days biking to where we thought he was located. It was clear that we were in a different phase. If the Germans had been angry before, they were outraged now.

THIRTEEN

DEATH AND DESTRUCTION

FOLLOWING THE ALLIED LANDINGS ON THE NORMANDY
coast on June 6, the French Resistance groups increased their efforts
to disrupt German communications and supply lines. In turn, the
German military, particularly those who had served on the eastern
front, ratcheted up their response to Resistance activity. Their brutality increased.

A clear demonstration of this took place at the village of Oradour-
sur-Glane on June 10. Although it was quite far south it did not escape German brutality, which was now a norm. It was hard to see
the violence increasing as the two sides battled for control. On this
day, an SS Panzer Division massacred 642 people—almost the entire population—and then destroyed the village. SS soldiers locked
the men in barns and the women and children in the church. They
then set fire to the barns and threw grenades through the windows
of the church, shooting anyone who sought to escape.

Finally, they looted the place and burned it to the ground.

Four days later, on June 14, General de Gaulle landed in Normandy, back in France. And on a much smaller scale, on June 16, I was promoted to Section Officer along with Sonia Butt (a courier) and my fellow radio operators Lilian Rolfe and Maureen O'Sullivan. The file notes say that the promotion was due to "the important operational work in the field and increasing responsibility." That would be about right. Everything had an urgency about it now, and everything had consequences.

✸ ✸ ✸

SOON AFTER D-DAY, I was sure that a laundry van I had spied was home to a direction-finder. I moved with speed to shut down and move out. For this sked I had chosen to use the big upright Morse key that came with the set instead of the smaller one I carried with me. If my messages looked different to the direction-finders because of the change in the key, they might think there was another person in the area. It was stupid of me really, as it cost me some time. I felt like I was courting capture that day.

They were on to the seats of bikes, too, and at one checkpoint I was told by a soldier that he had orders to search the seat of every bike. He looked at it, but all he saw were springs—I had done such a good job both of hiding the key and of hiding my emotions. You needed to remain calm and confident. If you showed any nerves, you were looked at more thoroughly. Inwardly you were scared, but outwardly you were unconcerned.

Katia and I did not find Claude where we expected him to be, but Séailles was there with his sidekick Mickey. Mickey was a womanizer, and when I saw him take a girl away who was plainly not amenable I felt terrible that I could not go to her rescue. I just left. If anything like that happened, I left. I couldn't risk being there in case the police or the Germans were called. Thankfully, another woman intervened and got the girl away from him.

Séailles was a bit of a bastard as well. He came to me one day, saying, "Krino is at that time of the month, and might you be kind to me?" Without waiting for my reply—which of course would have been "no"—he launched himself at me to kiss me and I fell into an old chair with him on top of me. I reacted with "Fiche le camp!" which means "Bugger off!"

Katia heard what was happening. She ran in with a bit of timber and hit Séailles on the back of his shoulder. She thought he was going to rape me. I thought he wasn't, but what he did still wasn't right.

When Claude got to hear about it later, he apparently punched Séailles, saying, "We'll have none of that stuff"—meaning "non-consensual" stuff. Given that Katia had supposedly been recruited by Lise "for her brother's pleasure," it must have made him most unhappy when I took her as my courier and left him with his sister! I never knew whether Katia and Claude spent time together when she was not with me. I suspect they did, but I never questioned Katia about it. She knew how to look after herself and what she wanted or didn't want. Life is always fleeting, but in wartime you can see this so clearly. Knowing that one of you might not be there at the end of the day, what might be normal in peacetime is different in wartime. To each their own, in any case.

At least, in that moment, Claude and I agreed on something: neither of us liked Séailles very much. After the war, Séailles's wife Krino told me that she had divorced him. I said, "Congratulations!"

★ ★ ★

THE DIRECTIVE FROM LONDON now was that we must attack intensively in our area, which was undertaken with fervor. Everywhere you looked, the landscape was a war zone, whether from Allied bombing, Resistance sabotage, or German warfare. Horse-drawn carts were blown to pieces; trucks lay exploded on bombed-out roads; towns and villages were reduced to rubble in parts. And there were so many dead people. I got used to seeing a lot of dead people, and weirdly I would often feel elated. "It's you lying there, not me," was my immediate thought. Now, people might not like hearing that sort of thing, but it was how I felt at the time. At the heart of it was self-preservation. I wanted to survive, and seeing dead people made you realize that there was no real separation between living and dying. A moment in time, that's all.

The battle for Normandy raged on as the Allies pushed forward. There was no shortage of equipment being dropped to arm those battling on the ground, as my regular communications with London attested. Katia and I decided to head back to Vire. It was here that I had occasion to use the S-Phone to speak directly to an incoming bomber. I "wore" the equipment, nicely covered by the newly requisitioned American poncho.

A "Jedburgh" special ops crew of three was being parachuted in from the bomber, and I deemed it unsafe for them to do so because they would have been picked off by the Germans who I knew were hiding nearby. The S-Phone required a line of sight to get a clear signal and I knew I would only have about a two-minute window to make contact. I judged my timing, then opened my comms with: "Suggest abort. There has been a betrayal. Will leave it up to you." I did not know for sure whether the drop would have been safe or not, but from my experience I reckoned the Gestapo were close and the jumpers could well be dead before they hit the ground.

"And who are you, Miss?" came an English voice in reply. I said I was Paulette, bade farewell, and shut down the connection as I watched them fly off without dropping their parachutists.

Many years later, the man I had spoken with that day confirmed that they had seen movement in the jump zone after receiving my warning, and were grateful that their men had not been dropped to their deaths. This man, Dick Rubenstein, tracked me down through the Special Forces Club, with only the name Paulette and the date from his logbook to go on, and we stayed in touch after the war.

* * *

DEATH ALSO CAME CALLING closer to home. One day in early July the news that came through via the couriers was shocking.

The word was that a woman wearing a blouse made from parachute silk had been arrested by the Gestapo, and the information she provided, likely confirmed by neighboring collaborators, culminated in the SS turning up at the home of Madame and Monsieur Grosclaude. This couple, who were out at the time, were in the Resistance and their farmhouse south of Caen provided a base for René and Vladimir (Maurice) to work from. A man called Jean Foucu, who was working with them, and a recently downed Canadian pilot—Harry Cleary—were also at the house at the time of the visit.

René answered the door, then went to get his identity information as asked, accompanied by one of the officers. Instead of his papers René grabbed a gun and turned it on the officer, killing him. A shoot-out ensued, in which another three SS men died and the farmhouse occupants made their escape. A further SS man was wounded in the skirmish, and his calls for help to a close-by German camp were, unfortunately, successful. Pursued by these soldiers, the group split up—René and Vladimir ran in one direction, and Foucu and Cleary in others.

Apparently René stumbled and was shot in the face, and although he fought hard was bundled into a car by the Gestapo, never to be seen again. He is presumed to have been executed. Vladimir was killed outright, and it was believed that Cleary was also tracked down and killed.

Foucu, however, lived to tell the tale. He made for Champgené- teux because René had told him if he was ever in trouble to go there and ask for Paulette or Claude, who might be staying with someone whose name started with B. Foucu could not recall the name, but it would have been Simone and Georges Baguenard. In any event Foucu did not connect with our team, although he did say in his report that he recognized my name only because we had met briefly after my May parachute drop and he was impressed by my courage.

Of course the Gestapo had Eugénie and Georges Grosclaude's home searched, and removed arms, explosives, and a radio set. The Grosclaudes were arrested, tortured, and, presumably, killed. Their orphaned children would likely have been shipped off to a convent to be raised there.

Soon afterward, word came from a twelve-year-old girl who helped on the farm about the woman with the parachute-silk blouse. She had been seen in the sidecar of a motorbike driven by an SS officer, which stopped beside a field. He must have said that he wasn't going to take her any farther—she'd done her job by giving him the information, so she should just make her way home from there. She would have stepped out thinking she was free—but then she was shot in the back and killed.

It was devastating news. Our two good young men, René and Maurice—aged just twenty and twenty-two, respectively—were dead. And, speaking practically, it meant another radio operator gone when we were already in short supply.

* * *

A FEW DAYS LATER I was going through a checkpoint some way north of Champgenéteux when I saw Simone behind me. Of course I did not show that I knew her. We had contact from time to time in various secretive, out-of-the-way places to exchange information and speak freely. It was always good to see Simone, even when we couldn't acknowledge each other in public. She always had her bonny little baby boy on her hip, who smiled away as if he had no worries in the world. Oh, to be a baby. It was good to see them outside of Paul's house and the baby looking so "well."

On this particular day, unbeknownst to me, Simone had seen a Frenchwoman who was known to be the mistress of a high-ranking SS officer, so followed the woman back to her home and reported her to Claude. He sent a squad to kidnap her, taking her to a forest to hide her away. Simone told him she had seen me talking to this woman at a checkpoint earlier in the day, so Claude got a message to me to come south straightaway to confirm the identification and pass on any information I might have gleaned. On the way, although I rode up to the checkpoints as usual, I took great care to hide my soap so that it looked like I had none. I had recently been through these checkpoints the other way, so did not want to arouse suspicion as to why I was coming back so soon. If I was asked, my story would be that I had unexpectedly run out of soap and was going back to collect more. I was fairly well known at most of the checkpoints, so my story needed to be believable.

By the time I arrived in the forest on the edge of the village a couple of days later, it must have been three or four days since the Frenchwoman had been kidnapped. The light was fading at the end of the day, with the curfew upon us. In the half light I could see that the woman was tied up, sitting against a tree with her back to me. Séailles was there too, standing guard, as was Mickey. Simone was standing beside Claude some way away from them, and I quietly joined them.

Claude started with the first of many questions. "Is that her?"

I crept around to a vantage point where I could see the woman without her seeing me, and returned to say it was. She looked exhausted, scared, and disheveled compared with the woman I had met a few days ago, but it was definitely her. Seeing her, I could feel the adrenaline starting to build in me—this was a messy situation that I had been brought into.

"What happened at the checkpoint?" was the next question. I gave him a detailed account, explaining that yes, I had talked to her at the checkpoint, but I did not know who she was. We just happened to be standing in line together, waiting to have our papers checked. I struck up a conversation, saying that I was going through to the next village to sell soap and asking her where she was going. She told me she was going into the countryside to look for food as a birthday gift for her man.

Simone said who they thought her lover was, and I realized I knew him—Katia and I had seen him about. He was a high-ranking SS officer who liked his meals. His girth was proof of that—no wonder she was off to find more food for him! We had personal experience of his love of food from the farmhouse he was billeted at. Katia and I were always on the hunt for used pea pods to put in our dinner cook-ups, but had given up on ever getting any from that farm. He must have been keeping most of the pea pods back to be turned into a soup for himself.

I told this to Claude and Simone, then returned to what had happened at the checkpoint. After the woman told me what she was doing, I reciprocated by telling her about the soap I was selling. She picked up a ball, and clearly liked the feel and smell of it, asking me if she could have some. I told her it wasn't possible because the Germans knew exactly how much I was bringing to sell to them—it was all part of the control they liked to exercise. I did offer to get some to her later if there was any left over, but she politely refused. And that was all we said to each other before parting ways.

Simone nodded her head in understanding, and Claude also seemed satisfied. He moved on to the issue they were trying to resolve. When interrogated, the woman kept saying she was a de Gaullist, but Claude was not convinced. "She is not—she is a collaborator," he stated emphatically.

I came up with what I thought might be a helpful suggestion. "Let me go and find a set, and I can use my emergency channel to find out what London knows about her."

He nodded in agreement before continuing with his next concern. "We can't hold her here much longer—her not being seen will be suspicious, let alone me being out of circulation as well. The

Germans will wonder where we are. You need to get help." I figured that this meant finding someone else to take Claude's place. I said, "Okay, leave it with me," and promptly headed out of the forest with the two duties I needed to achieve. Claude and I were working nicely as a team, I thought. The adrenaline was kicking in properly now. I needed to find trusted help and get on the air to London quickly and quietly. There was no time to waste and no mistakes to be made.

As I walked, I mused on why Claude had not just dispensed with the woman. He was known to be very handy with that requirement. He must have deemed her useful alive—maybe he could get some valuable information out of her. I'm sure he had concluded that she wouldn't go straight home to her lover and rat on them. If she did talk, the SS officer would know that she was now compromised and he would have no trouble putting a bullet in her.

I was almost out of the forest when I heard a shot. Séailles, the bastard, had shot her—I knew it was him because he hadn't used a silencer. Claude was an old hand with a gun, and he always conducted himself tidily with a silencer. I backtracked a little to assess the scene. As I had feared, things were truly messy now. The woman was slumped over and Séailles was picking himself up off the ground, spoiling for a fight. Claude, who had punched him, was plainly enraged with Séailles.

"Do you not think? Your stupidity will bring the Germans. And"—he continued—"it will be me who is executed, not you!" I couldn't tell from where I was whether the woman had been killed from the back or the front. If the front, I think she would have tried to grab the gun, so it seemed likely that Séailles had shot her in the back of the head. What they did with her body was their problem, and my plans had also immediately changed. I needed to get some manpower to come to their aid quickly. If the Germans had heard the gunshot, they would be here soon. I knew where they were, and it was close by to where I knew I could get the help we needed.

I cycled to two farms where teenage boys lived next door to each other. They were in a reserved occupation, needed on the farms to provide food for the Germans, so weren't in danger of being taken away as forced labor. As I was supposedly a teenage girl, they had already introduced themselves to me, and as part of my alias I had even entertained the odd kiss and cuddle from them. But given that I was really twenty-three, a liaison with a fifteen- or sixteen-year-old was never going to happen. They were just kids, even though one of them was trying to grow a mustache. Imagine if they had known I was twenty-three.

Within fifteen minutes of leaving the forest I had taken a couple of Sten guns and ammunition from a hidden stash I knew about from a recent drop. I suspected that the boys might want to stay out of the goings-on, but the weaponry might be a sweetener. "If you come and help me," I said to them both, "you can keep the Sten guns, and the belt with cartridges." Accepting the offer of weaponry, they quickly followed me on their bikes back to the scene. It was nighttime but we all knew the roads well.

When we got to the area, we found that the Germans had just turned up and were starting to shoot indiscriminately. They were on the higher ground in front of us with Claude's group trapped beyond them in the valley below, hiding in the dark. I thought it would be best to draw the attention of the Germans away from the forest floor. I placed the boys in a position where we were lined up nicely to shoot over the heads of the Germans.

"Kill nobody," I briefed the boys, "just start shooting at them from behind, over their heads. If we kill even one of them, we will have a lot of hostages taken and we don't want that."

The moment the Germans heard shots come from behind them, they ceased shooting and did not move. Our hiding place was working perfectly to our advantage, but I told the boys: "Now they've stopped, don't use the machine gun. Fire single shots at them. But make sure you keep missing them." My hope was that they might think we were snipers. Of course in reality we were shooting at nothing, but it was important to maintain regular fire to keep them concerned.

While the Germans were distracted with the "snipers" behind them, Claude took his chance and got his group out. They had spent the time while I was away getting help to put the body under a fallen trunk and camouflage the burial place so it would be unlikely ever to be found. There would be no other evidence to find, either.

A few minutes later, we left quickly. The boys rode home safely (with their guns) and I cycled off in a different direction to find a new piece of forest to bed down in for the remainder of the night. As I tucked myself under my American poncho, I wondered whether Séailles would be pleased with himself because he could now say he had killed a traitor. In my mind, as well as that of others', it was not worth it. His act of vanity could have gotten us all killed.

★ ★ ★

AS THE SUMMER WORE on, the Allies kept moving through France and the Germans kept pushing back. Saint-Lô, which I knew quite well by now, was just a derelict mess by mid-July when the Americans liberated it. The scenes were jubilant, the locals thrilled with the victors. I recall being in a throng of people when an American scooped me up in his arms and put me on his tank for a photograph. It was emotional to see such relief on people's faces and hear what happiness sounded like. I had almost forgotten.

The moments of elation were interspersed with the outing and public humiliation of collaborators. Women like the lover of the SS officer—had she survived Séailles's ego—would have been one of those shamed. "Les femmes tondues" were female collaborators whose heads were shaved in a very public event. There could be no hiding in full view then. Everyone would know at a glance what they had done.

While liberation was sweeping its way through France, those SOE women who had been captured were beginning to be dealt with by the Germans at POW camps in Germany. Andrée Borrel, Vera Leigh, and Sonia Olschanezky had all been arrested in Paris—Andrée in June 1943, Vera in November 1943, and Sonia in January 1944—and Diana Rowden was captured near Clairvaux-les-Lacs in November 1943. They had been held at Karlsruhe Prison in Germany before being moved to the Natzweiler-Struthof concentration camp in eastern France on July 6, 1944—this was the only such camp located on French soil. The Alsace region, where the camp was, had returned to French hands after World War I, but in this second war the Germans had again occupied it. Andrée, Vera, Sonia, and Diana were killed on the same day they arrived at the camp—injected with phenol, which was supposedly lethal, then incinerated in the ovens at the crematorium. Sadly, they would not be the last of the executions. It was probably better that I did not know of any of these events at the time. The stark reality of the price one could pay for the job could well have been an all-encompassing, paralyzing thought.

Muriel Byck, a fellow radio operator, worked in the Loir-et-Cher area. She was not captured, but died on May 23, 1944, of meningitis. She passed away in a hospital in Romorantin, in the arms of Philippe de Vomécourt, her organizer in the Ventriloquist network.

* * *

I JUST KEPT DOING what I was doing—selling soap, gathering intelligence, sending messages, and keeping my head down, both for my own sake and for that of the people I knew. I didn't want to put my "grandparents" at risk by staying with them when I was in the area, as tempting as that thought was, so the nature of Normandy was my bed every night. There were plenty of places to sleep, although German tanks and army personnel would often hide in the larger forests so we had to be careful about our selection of sleeping spots. Sometimes a tank would unexpectedly pop out of a forest, ideally *not* when we were lying on the road with our ears to the ground listening for the rumble of army transport. On a couple of occasions we were indeed doing just that, but fortunately the tank turned the other way. Thoroughly relieved, we scampered to a spot hidden from view to recover and celebrate the odds being in our favor.

Where there were German tanks, there were typically SS, and reporting on tank positions became a regular communication from me. In one of my skeds I had reported three tanks hiding in a forested area, then (as always) moved quickly away before the area was bombed. Not only was this for my own safety, but also so that no pattern could be established between my being in the area and those places being bombed soon afterward. On this occasion I had put "No Yanks" in my message, because in my experience they stayed too high and were therefore not precise enough in their bombing. They were unlike the Polish, who swooped in low and made a tidy job of it. I was pleased to see that the Poles were used for that forest, because there were a lot of civilians in surrounding villages who would have been harmed if the bombing was not done accurately.

The following day, however, I heard that a grandmother had gone into the forest to pick mushrooms with her two grandchildren, and they had all been wiped out in the low-level precision bombing. It was all my doing and I felt terrible. Worse still, my "grandparents" knew the family. I was in Champgenéteux to get more soap and they told me about the tragedy. A funeral had been arranged, which my "grandparents" were planning to attend. The whole village would be turning out. The Durands said that I should go, too, not only as a mark of respect but also because it would look very odd if their granddaughter did not come—it could be construed as suspicious.

I did not want to cause my "grandparents" any trouble, so I went. It was very confronting to see the raw grief displayed and know that I was the cause of it. Nobody knew that the "assassin" was at the funeral. It was a secret that I kept very much to myself.

☆ ☆ ☆

ONE MORNING A FEW days later, Katia and I had awoken from our forest slumber and were talking about where we would meet that night when we heard a German truck rumble by. We quickly got going and tracked it to where it had stopped on the other side of the forest, hiding ourselves some distance away to see what was going on.

Eight people, five men and three women, were removed from the truck and lined up. I knew what was going to happen next. These were hostages, who would have been randomly picked up in the streets of a local village that morning as retribution for a German soldier dying somewhere in the vicinity in the past few days. The Germans would often wait for a market day, then swoop in and grab people at random. Some poor person would find themselves in the wrong place at the wrong time and be manhandled into a German truck. It would have been chaos. This was another reason why I stayed away from villages.

Eight shots rang out, and eight people fell. Then the officer went past them all and, regardless of whether they were dead or not, gave them the coup de grâce in the back of the head. He was cold and efficient. I could see him linger over one of the women's bodies, because she had fallen in a different position from the others. He used his boot on her face to turn her over, then kicked her around a bit more to get her where he wanted before shooting her. I hoped that the first bullet had killed her outright.

During my time in France, I was usually of the mindset that I simply couldn't worry about distressing things like this. It was done, and it couldn't be undone. But the way that officer treated this particular woman upset both me and Katia. There was no dignity in death being offered here. Then something switched in me, and I found myself moving quickly to my usual feeling of "I'm glad it is you lying there, not me"—my go-to defense mechanism that allowed me to stay sane.

At the end of that day, when we had time together in a safe place, Katia and I got to talking about the loss of René and Maurice. She had been used to seeing René and Lise regularly, exchanging information courier to courier for Maurice or me to transmit to London. We reflected on what a loss they were, both to us personally and to the Scientist network.

We sat with our somber thoughts, saying nothing for a while. When Katia broke the silence, it was to bring me into her confidence. "I need to tell you something that René told me recently. It's about you."

I leaned forward, intrigued, as she continued: "He said that Claude told him he wanted Maurice to send a message to London to have you recalled." She paused. "I think it might have been me that set him off, though."

"What did you say about me?" I asked, in some trepidation.

"Nothing bad, of course! It was just that I refused to tell Claude where you were—he often asked me. And I always refused because, as your courier, I am the only one who needs to know where you are. He didn't like that."

I was aghast. How long before he died had Maurice sent that message? And, more importantly, what was the reply?

"What did home station say?" I asked Katia, thinking that she must know.

She replied with a smile that instantly put me at ease. "René said that Maurice didn't send the message—because he thought it wasn't right."

Claude, however, thought that it had gone. I wondered what Claude thought about me now. I had just come to his rescue, so maybe I was now okay in his book. Regardless, London never got the message. Good old Maurice.

I found out much later that the loss of Maurice as his radio operator made Claude even less enamored of me. He did finally get an unfavorable message about me back to London a good month or so later, using another network (Toddler). The message itself seems not to have survived the war, but it is referenced in my file:

Scientist Report, L35, August 1944

GENEVIEVE

I am sorry to say that GENEVIEVE did not prove comparable in any way to VLADIMIR. I do not wish, after the work done and which is now over, which she accomplished with stupidity but also with courage, to take from her the little merit which she deserves, but would merely refer back to my telegram through TODDLER, where I gave a full report of her activities.

Thanks, Claude. Very good of you.

* * *

WE HAD A COUPLE more incidents on our way back to the wider area around Champgenéteux. On one occasion we found ourselves in some ruins when the Gestapo came to investigate the nearby farmhouse. We had not started to assemble the set yet, which was fortunate timing as it allowed us to scramble out the back of the building and onto the top of it. Katia and I stayed hidden up there for what seemed like an age as they searched the farmhouse and the ruins out the back. Thankfully, the half-ruined roof cloaked us sufficiently. We were lucky that day.

Another time I was sending in a ruinous old building behind another farmhouse when a German officer entered. He couldn't see me in the dark because I was right at the back, but things could easily have changed if he had stayed put. Thankfully, he was quickly enticed out of there by the farmer's daughter offering him a glass of cider. I had clocked up a couple of lucky escapes in short order.

My good luck would soon run out. Following another hostage shooting, I went to check on the bodies to see if any of "our lot" were in there. Thankfully they were not. I was almost back to where I had left my bike when I saw two young German soldiers walking toward me. They can't have been any older than seventeen or eighteen. Something felt wrong—I didn't like the way they were looking at me and whispering to each other, but I made myself pass them confidently. Had they seen me in the forest? Did they suspect I was not who I purported to be? My nerves were threatening to get the better of me. It was wearing to be living in a constant state of fear of getting caught—it was always there at the back of my mind. I sighted Katia in the distance and my mood changed in an instant. It was always reassuring to see her. We had grown quite close.

I gave myself a silent talking-to—of course all was well. Except that suddenly it wasn't. I had not walked far beyond the men when I heard a scuffle. One of them grabbed me roughly from behind, covering my mouth as he dragged me toward a doorway. The other pushed the door open as I was manhandled inside. Suddenly it dawned on me what their intent was: rape. I was scared—very scared—the adrenaline coursing through me. I was determined not to be an easy prospect for them, but before I knew it I was on the ground. As much as I struggled to push away the man holding me down for his comrade, there were two of them and only one of me. It was useless. One of them forcibly kissed me on the lips—and from that day forward I have never allowed anyone to kiss me on my lips. He ruined that for me.

Their roughness made me realize I might be better not to fight as much—that way, it would be over sooner. It was a desolate feeling to know that help would not come.

Katia, though, had seen me get attacked and pushed into the building. Neither of us would usually interact with the authorities when we saw women being assaulted, but on this occasion Katia could not stand by and do nothing. She ran up to an SS officer who happened to not be far away and pleaded with him to help a young schoolgirl who was being raped by two soldiers. The answer she got was extraordinary—but not surprising: "Leave her," he said, before brushing her aside and walking on. "They will give her good strong German sons."

Katia knew that if she came to my aid herself, the SS officer could have killed her for disobeying him. She must have felt utterly helpless. Fortunately, soon after the SS man had gone out of sight, she spotted a German army officer and his driver. Determined to try again to get me some help, she flagged down the car, pointed toward the building I was in, and said: "A schoolgirl is being raped in there and the SS won't help." Unlike the SS officer, the army man did come to my aid, opening the car door and signaling for his driver to join him.

By this time, I had given up on any sort of rescue and was feeling numb to what was going on. Suddenly, the door burst open and a shaft of light fell upon the dark, dank scene. I saw a German officer striding in purposefully, another man hot on his heels. In that instant my heart sank: Was there more for me to endure? But the officer pulled out his gun and shot one of the offending men, and his companion quickly followed suit with the other rapist. *Boom, boom,* both men dead. There I was, lying on the floor, with one dead man on either side of me.

The German officer put his gun away, took his scarf off, and knelt close to me. As he gently wiped my face, in silence, with the scarf, it felt like a kind thing to do. "Go home," he said in a quiet voice when he had finished. Then he and his driver left.

It's a bit of a blur as to what happened immediately after that, but I do recall that a photo was taken. I know somebody was there, I just don't know who or why. I should have asked Katia what that was about—she had come in after hearing shots fired and was tending to me—but I was clearly in shock.

Dear Katia got me out of there and we spent the night in a secluded forest not far away. I felt safest away from people, and safest with just her. As I was trying to quieten my mind to get to sleep, though, a feeling of guilt crept over me. I was responsible for the deaths of those men because the German army officer had thought I was fourteen. I doubted that he would have come to my aid if he had known I was twenty-three, and they would both still be alive. What they did to me was abhorrent—no question—but now, perversely, I felt at fault.

The next day we went to Paul's house in Bais because I was worried that I could be pregnant, and he gave me a rather late douche. Thankfully I turned out not to be, but that was only part of it. Those young soldiers had roughed me up. I had been quite hurt while they were trying to open my legs and I was resisting. I certainly needed a few days under Paul's expert care to repair physically. Emotional repair was harder, and would take much longer. On top of all the other things I had to contend with, I now felt unsafe on my own around men I did not know.

FOURTEEN

TIME TO LEAVE

AS SOON AS THE MONTH OF AUGUST STARTED, THINGS moved up a gear. In one of my skeds I got an abnormally long message from London—twenty minutes of fierce writing when any other time it would be more like five minutes. By the time I had finished, I couldn't write anymore. I later made a complaint about it—it was dangerous to be on the air for as long as I was that day.

When I decoded the message, there was a lot to take in. I was told that this might be the last time I would hear from them. The liberation of Paris was inevitable, and I was to get out and make for Paris from where I would be flown back to England. I had to make myself known to the Allies using the appropriate codes and identifying information. The Americans, given that they were in the area, had been told to give assistance to any SOE personnel needing to get out of the war zone. And I couldn't get out without a pass—this would need to be issued by them.

The same went for Katia. The end was in sight, it seemed. We just had to make it to Paris.

* * *

CLAUDE AND LISE WERE nowhere to be seen, so Katia and I were on our own now. We decided to make for Champgenéteux, which was close, because I wanted to connect with Simone one last time and see my "grandparents." I also wanted to see Paul in Bais.

The area where they all lived had become home to a high-stakes retaliatory game. In the first few days of August the Resistance attacked multiple German targets daily. In what had become the usual way, a local priest and multiple hostages were killed in retaliation. The Germans also attempted to set fire to a farmhouse in Bais, where the man living there had been blind from birth. He was shot dead by a burst of machine-gun fire before they fled. In retribution for this, later the same day the Resistance killed several Germans in the local area. They even set up a temporary POW facility guarded by Russian deserters and supervised by the Resistance. In an unfortunate accident, the RAF also bombed a convoy of refugees they had mistaken for Germans. It was chaotic, with death everywhere.

Paul's car was stopped and searched by the SS. He explained that some blood on his shirt resulted from him attending a birth and even showed them the forceps he'd used, but they didn't believe him. They had him lined up at the end of their guns when, thankfully, a German officer who knew Paul stepped in and stopped them. He got in the car with Paul to drive home with him, and on the way asked, in poor French, if Paul could please forgive his men for the near-death experience. He offered the reason that, exhausted by the sheer volume of terrorist attacks by the Resistance, they had become a bit trigger-happy. When the officer left Paul's car, at the entrance to Bais, Paul decided not to go home but to instead drive to his mother's house. This was a fortunate decision. There, Paul was told to flee immediately because his home had just been surrounded. His name had been given to the SS by the local drunk of the town.

Paul spent the night in the nearby forest before traveling by foot to his mother's abandoned farmhouse, La Roisière, on the outskirts of Champgenéteux. He had sensibly sent his wife and two children there forty-eight hours previously, having seen the increasing violence on both sides. La Roisière would become Paul's base until the liberating forces had passed through and things settled down. He abandoned his trusty car because it was so well known, and from then on his only transport was a bike.

It was into this sort of volatile environment that I came to say goodbye to Simone. I told her what I had heard from London. We both knew from the chaos happening around the area that things were on a knife-edge.

"I need to leave," I told her, knowing that she of all people would understand.

"Yes, you need to go," she said.

I hoped that things would be okay for her, and that she, Georges, and their little boy would be safe whatever this next period of conflict threw at them. They were brave patriots who had fought hard and risked their lives on numerous occasions for the cause of liberation, and they deserved happiness and peace. "Thank you for everything," I said. "You have been so important to me."

The little boy was eleven months old now and almost walking. "You'll miss his first birthday," Simone said with a warm smile.

"Yes, I will," I replied, "but the lucky boy will have the best gift of all—a liberated France."

"And better health, too," she added. "He won't be needing as many doctor's visits."

We shared a laugh, and the little boy sensed the lightened mood and chuckled too. He, thankfully, wouldn't remember any of this.

When I asked Simone for the gold pen from Buckmaster and the gold powder compact from Vera, her reply stunned me. "Claude has them—he said he would take them back to England for you."

This did not seem like a kindness Claude would offer, but it was not for me to burden Simone with my suspicions. She went on to tell me that one of the local farm boys was visiting at the time and could corroborate the discussion between Simone and Claude. I would sort it out back in London, I decided. I just had to get there first. Saying farewell, I turned and left Simone with her little boy on her hip. Much like when I had first met her.

In the surrounding area, many of the farmers had gone. That included my "grandparents"—they had fled south, not wanting to be in the line of fire. My set was still there, so I used it to let London know I was leaving. It wasn't a normal sked time, of course, so I sent as an "emergency." The brief message said that I was leaving Champgenéteux. "ETA Paris IMI." IMI was the three-letter radio code for a question mark—I had no idea when I would get to Paris. I closed the set without giving them time to answer, and gathered a stash of Benzedrine tablets, thinking I would need to stay alert on the road to Paris. It was a long walk in peacetime—it would be a very long walk in wartime.

As I left the house, the neighboring farmer recognized me and waved. Unlike others, he had decided to stay. There was no conversation about where my "grandparents" were or what my plans were. I think he knew what I was about, but did not let on. He gave me a gentle hug and looked at me closely to make sure I took in his parting words. "Be careful, Paulette, very careful."

My last stop was to see Paul at La Roisière. He looked tired. Ours was a quick farewell, because we both knew I needed to get on the road and out of there before I was caught. We didn't need to say much, anyway. Paul had always had my back, and it was hard to think about what we had been through together in the past three months. It seemed so much longer than that. I first met him on May 2, 1944, and I was saying goodbye on August 8. I would never see him again.

* * *

KATIA AND I HAD decided to head to the area around Vire, to the north toward Caen. We wanted to avoid the heat of the conflicts by going in afterward to connect with people who could, hopefully, help get us out. Saint-Lô and Vire had been liberated by the Americans, and Caen by the British. We knew we would get help somewhere around there. Katia and I then parted ways, thinking we would be wise to travel separately and knowing we would see each other at some point on the nominated exit route. She went ahead.

All three of these towns were ones we had spent time in over the past three months, and to see the devastated state of them was sobering. Being at the junction of several roads and railways, Caen represented a strategic win for both sides. The land south of Caen is flatter and more open than the area north and west of it, which was attractive to the Allied air-force commanders—they could then base more aircraft in France. The city had been a target ever since D-Day, when much of the town was on fire from the Allied bombardment, and continued to be so thereafter. I had seen the smoke from Caen in my travels following D-Day, and knew it would only get worse until one side captured it fully. By the end, it was completely destroyed by a combination of constant bombing by the Allies alongside intense ground combat, which led to a huge number of French civilian casualties. After the battle, very little of the prewar city remained, and the reconstruction of the city would take another twenty years.

Vire was south of Caen and had been liberated by the Americans on August 7. It was here that Katia and I thought we would have the best chance of getting our tickets out. We knew from London's message that SOE had warned the Americans that they still had agents in the field and requested that if they identified themselves, the Americans should offer any assistance needed. I had my identity papers, codes, and names ready, as the Americans would need to connect with London to verify who I was so that they could supply the necessary pass to travel to Paris safely, avoiding mined roads.

The roads around Vire showed damage from tanks—ruined vegetation and branches ripped off trees by the vehicles making their way through the landscape. The sharp branches were the death knell for one young Frenchman who, I saw, had been impaled on a tree branch like a piece of meat on a skewer. He was still alive—barely—clutching a photo in his hand. I was just going to pass him and keep walking—after all, what could I do? Nothing. He was just waiting to die.

But then I thought I would give him some hope. I leaned down and whispered, "Hang on, the ambulance is on the way." I knew it wasn't true, that he would be dead soon, but he gave what I took to be a weak smile and I went on. It crossed my mind that I did not feel as disturbed as I probably should have. Seeing death had become so normal.

Then, within five minutes of seeing the poor young man, I came across a dead horse—and found myself crying, even wailing at volume. I got down on my knees and hugged the horse. It had flies on it, and I was batting them away, running my hands through its beautiful coat, rearranging its mane. The horse's body was warm, so it had only died recently. The poor thing had probably escaped in fright from a local farm and been hit by a tank. It had not asked for war. It had just been minding its own business and hadn't known what was going on. It was really so strange. I could feel nothing for a dying human being; I'd seen so many. But a dead animal had me in an emotional spin.

Just before I entered Vire itself, I found a ruined building where I thought I might have a little rest, and remarkably I managed to sleep for a while. These days I never seemed to sleep deeply anymore or for any length of time, but the shade provided by the ruins made it a good spot for a quick catnap. When I woke up, I saw a German soldier sleeping not too far away from me. He had not been there when I went to sleep, and I was horrified to think that I had not awoken when he arrived.

I looked for a gun, but could not see one. I don't know what his story is and why he is here, I thought to myself, but I don't think he is a threat.

As I quietly stood up to leave, he woke up. We looked at one another—it was quite a surreal moment—but he did not do anything to make me think he was in any way threatening. I saw him looking at the stocking I was carrying, with three turnips in it, and then quickly look away.

"You have this food," I said. He shook his head.

"No," I insisted, "you have the food. I'll get food when I reach the Americans and the Allies. You won't get food."

I gave him all I had, and left.

* * *

LIKE MOST OF THE other towns in Normandy, Vire was a bombed-out mess. When I finally found the American HQ, it was because I was following my nose—quite literally. An enticing smell of food led me to a group of men cooking a meal for their troops.

The first man I spoke to looked me up and down—presumably because of what I was wearing.

"Yes, I have been sleeping outside," I said, "and yes, the American poncho was stolen—sorry." Having gotten that out of the way, I followed up with the reason I was there.

"I think this is where I report in. I need to speak to someone in Intelligence."

"Sure, ma'am," came the laconic reply.

I followed him to a tent, where a US Army officer asked to look at my papers, and he in turn took them to another officer before coming back with an answer I did not expect.

"We will need to detain you here with us, while we sort this out."

They could not verify my identity. The papers I offered were those of a fourteen-year-old soap-seller from the Belgian Congo via Paris, but back in London my alias was still listed as a twenty-nine-year-old professional secretary from Lyon. Quite different! Because I had failed to tell London about my new alias when Paul changed it, I was now paying the price for my administrative oversight. I was not sure where this would end up. I really needed someone on the France end of things to reassure them, but that was next to impossible.

I was taken to a broken-down ambulance and told I needed to stay there while they made more inquiries. I was, effectively, under arrest and their prisoner. The ambulance was guarded, and it was plain that I was now under American control and not going anywhere until this was sorted out.

I must have been sitting there for an hour or so, wondering what would happen next, when out of nowhere a man turned up. Introducing himself as Giles, he said he knew of me because he knew Katia.

"Do you know where she is?" I asked.

"No, I am sorry I do not," he answered, "but I would presume she has already secured a pass and has already gone."

Giles told me he could probably get this identity thing ironed out for me. It was like I had been sent a fairy godmother. I had no idea, though, how he fitted into things. He had a French accent, but there was something unusual about him that I couldn't put my finger on. Was he MI6? He could be. Was he Russian? I suspected he might be. Was he SOE? Not sure. Would I ever know? Probably not. From the interactions I saw, however, it was obvious that the Americans knew him and trusted him, and that was the most important thing.

Giles asked for some food for us, which we received in a little tin. He told me that sorting things out might take a day or so, and to utilize the bed in the ambulance. I was shattered and even having had an afternoon nap I fell asleep quickly. Perhaps it was because I was lying on a bed—I was not used to such a thing. In the twilight zone before sleep overtook me, I remembered a cushion being put under my head and a blanket placed over me. It was so foreign to be receiving such kindness.

When I woke a couple of hours later, the ubiquitous Giles was there again (had he ever left?) with good news. At this point it had been five hours since I had arrived.

"Everything is fine now; you are no longer detained. I have vouched for your identity." He gave me the all-important travel pass provided by the Americans, and suggested I join a group of refugees that was about to leave the city. On foot, of course. Before we left, a soldier talked to us about how far we could go each day—the days were still long and the nights short—and suggested places where we might stop for the night.

The others in the group were also making for Paris. We were warned that we must use our passes to follow the safest routes, which were not always the quickest routes. I could see on the map the soldier was showing us that the intended direction would take us back up to the coast for parts of it. This was because these areas were now under Allied control.

It was probably going to take us six to eight weeks if we did it all on foot, although there might be vehicular help from the Allies closer to Paris. Liberation of the capital city was close.

★ ★ ★

AS THE GROUP OF twenty or so started to head off, seeming satisfied with the instructions, Giles turned to me and said, "Okay, away you go now." This time with Giles had been strange—somehow he seemed to be my gatekeeper to a ticket to freedom from the chaos. I thanked him, walked off to collect my bike from another American soldier who had put it away safely, then pushed it out of the secure area toward the refugee group that had set off. I wondered how many miles I had done around Normandy on this bike in the past few months. Hundreds. It was now going on a last one-way journey with me.

I was just about to jump on and start pedaling when a young man came out of nowhere and tried to take the bike off me. I pulled it back, saying, "No! This is mine, you can't have it." We started to tussle over it—and then he hit me on the head. It was a fairly hard clout and all but knocked me over.

That was a shock, but what happened next was more so. From behind me, someone shot the man square in the face. He crumpled to the ground while I stood there, speechless.

"Look at his hand—he had a knife," came a familiar voice. It was Giles. He had seen what was happening and promptly dealt with the threat.

"He's not what you think," he went on. I had presumed he was a local refugee. "The Germans are throwing away their uniforms and stealing civilian clothes to get out of here, too. Be careful."

The group who had left were already out of sight. Giles waved in their direction. "You need to go."

I went. Somehow I found energy I did not know I possessed, and pedaled quickly to catch the group up. When I had almost reached them, I abandoned my bike by the side of the road and walked on to join the people at the back. I wasn't going to have any more fights over a bike, which was clearly a hot commodity. It was safer to walk.

The route we were taking went past the ruins where I had woken to see the German soldier. Glancing over, I saw a pair of legs sticking out of the ruins. Perhaps he had fallen asleep again—perhaps he had been wounded and I hadn't noticed? My curiosity took me back into the ruins. The soldier was slumped up against the walls, dead. He had been shot in the chest. The Allies must have come through and seen him there, not armed or anything, and killed him. It made me angry. He was harmless. He looked like he was only about seventeen. I could see that he had eaten all my turnips, though, which did allow me a small moment of happiness before the anger returned.

✷ ✷ ✷

OUR GROUP WAS ALL ages. I hung around toward the back where I befriended an older woman who told me her name was Bertha. We had been walking companions for a day or so when I heard the engine of a fighter aircraft coming up behind us. Everything in me froze. The sound of the mighty Merlin engine is beautiful when it is on your side, but not when the Spitfire has *you* in its gunsights. Surely, I thought, they can see we are refugees? But apparently not—for some reason the pilot thought we were a group of Germans escaping, and was intent on strafing the lot of us.

In a split second, everyone recognized the danger and most people panicked. I grabbed Bertha's arm and spun around to face the incoming aircraft and run toward it. It seemed counterintuitive but I knew it was the right thing to do—run back, not forward in the same direction as the artillery fire coming from the aircraft. Most of the group did run forward, seemingly away from the threat, which is a completely natural thing to do.

As the Spitfire came over, it opened up its guns. There were bodies strewn all over the road. Only a small handful of people had survived, us included. I motioned to Bertha that we should get off the road and go up through a field that had stock in it. From my training, I knew that that way would not be mined. Bertha was reluctant at first, because she only trusted the areas the Allies had marked "mine-free" with signs after they had cleared them. However, *I* knew that those signs were not to be trusted. I had seen both Germans and French move those signs to fields that did have mines in them. You could never trust the humans. You could only trust the animals.

It felt good to walk through the field among the animals, peaceful and calming after our lucky escape. As the day drew to a close, I found a place in a forested area for us to sleep for the night and we both fell asleep quickly.

I woke with the sunlight, and as I opened my eyes my first thought was how Bertha had slept after the trauma of the previous day. She didn't rouse with the first shake, so I made the second one a bit firmer—but soon saw that something was amiss. Her face was slack, with no expression. She had died. Bertha had no obvious injuries—I had checked that yesterday. Perhaps the shock had been too much for her. This little forested area seemed a peaceful place to leave her in as her last resting place; not that I had known it would be.

Before leaving, I took Bertha's shoes. Mine were barely any use anymore and very uncomfortable. The new shoes were a bit big for me, and I could see as I took them off Bertha that they had been a bit big for her too. She had told me she had taken them off a dead person she came across on the side of the road. And now the cycle was repeated. These shoes, I hoped, were now with their last owner. It surely could not be far now to Paris.

I rolled Bertha over so the birds would not peck at her eyes, and left to find the main road and a group to join.

★ ★ ★

LIFE ON THE ROAD got harder as time went on. Days merged into weeks, and the only constants were the rise and fall of the sun and the need for water. Most groups of people were on foot; there was the occasional one with a horse and cart. The only other traffic seemed to be military and we would just move to the side of the road and wait until they passed.

I did not always stay with the same group. Sometimes when they stopped to sleep at night, I would choose to walk farther on. I assumed that Katia must be somewhere on the road ahead of me and I wanted to try to catch up to her. She would be using the same pass as I had gotten from the Americans, which limited our routes, so I was hopeful I would find her somewhere along the way. Besides which, I wanted to get to Paris as quickly as I could. There were rumors that it had been freed (this happened on August 25), and I knew that if I got there, I could get back to England. There was another possibility, though: that Katia had died or been captured by the Germans—but I didn't want to think about that too much.

There was no food. The farms were empty—all of the people had left, either because their farms had been ruined by bombs or because they had no food themselves to eat. Others, concerned about conflict coming their way, were looking for refuge in some imagined utopia and joined the exodus. Yet others were already dead. You did not know which it was. You took what you could from the farms, but because the Germans had been there first there was little to find. Previously I had been pretty good at finding turnips, but even those were scarce now. A goose was seen one day, and three men in the group I was with began fighting over who could capture it.

In the end, it escaped their clutches. Farmers usually took a couple of feathers out to stop their geese flying away, but this one had obviously been without a farmer for a while because it did take flight.

When you don't eat, you eventually get to a stage where you don't want food. Plus, finding food takes time and energy, neither of which I had much of. I did have water—at the bottom of Normandy's big ditches there was usually water that looked quite clear. I would scoop it out with my hands and try to satiate myself that way. I would also keep a good eye out for a farm well where I could pump some water, and on a couple of occasions I even got a change of clothing from the odd thing left swinging on a makeshift clothesline. All I had was what I was standing in and a pair of worn-out shoes.

I slept mainly in forests, but there wasn't much actual sleep even though I was utterly exhausted. The Benzedrine supply I had brought from Champgenéteux helped me stay awake. I took one every couple of days. It was hard, though, the lack of sleep. I sometimes felt I was walking chin-first—leaning forward and willing the rest of me to follow behind. The idea of a long, deep sleep seemed an impossibility.

On one occasion the group I was with stopped to rest during the day, but with the Benzedrine in me I decided to walk ahead and find another group. It was always safest to be in a group, and although I couldn't see one right now, I knew another wouldn't be far away. And sure enough, within half an hour I saw one just ahead. It looked like a fight was going on, though, so I stayed back until it was over, not wanting to be involved. The group moved off, leaving this one chap lying on the ground. When I reached him, I could see he had been beaten to death.

He was bleeding everywhere around his head, and through his

mouth, and part of the skin had come off his face. One of his eyes had popped out of its socket and was hanging down his cheek. I've seen that eye in my dreams quite a bit since that day. When you see something like that, you can never unsee it.

He was one of the young men Giles had warned me about. The group knew he had changed sides for his own convenience and he was not one of them. He was wearing French civilian clothes—and should have found French shoes, or gone without, rather than keep his German boots on. Those boots now belonged to someone in the group ahead. German leather was hardy, which was good on a long walk, but it struck me that whoever was wearing them now would have to stay in known company or they could meet the same ugly fate as this young man.

★ ★ ★

IT MUST HAVE BEEN mid-September when we got to Falaise. A huge battle had been waged here in late August in which the Allies had encircled and destroyed a substantial part of the German forces. By the time I got there you could smell the place five or six miles away. The closer I got, the worse it smelled. There were dead men everywhere, and I mean *everywhere*—thousands of them. And horses. I wanted to cry when I saw the horses, but I was so exhausted (and dehydrated, probably) that even though I felt the huge welling of emotion that comes with crying, there were no tears. I simply stood there, stunned. There they were, still hitched up to their wagons, gunned down in a corridor of death. Once more, these poor animals were in a war not of their making. I had seen a lot of death in the past few months, but it was the animals that really got to me. I hated people for what they did to animals. It took about a week for the group I was with to walk through the Falaise area—like so much of this journey the route was not a straight line, and we walked many more miles than you would have done before the war. The Benzedrine was a great help. We had to get through as quickly as we could because you could hardly breathe with the terrible smell. For years afterward, I could smell it in my hair—I even had my locks cut short to get the smell out. And everybody would say to me, "There's no smell." And I would say, "There is. I can smell it. It's the smell of death."

I learned later that, while I was in Falaise, four more of my SOE F Section female compatriots were executed in Germany. Yolande Beekman, Madeleine Damerment, Noor Inayat-Khan, and Eliane Plewman were shot in the back of the head at Dachau concentration camp on September 13, 1944. Noor had survived in captivity the longest, having been arrested in October 1943 in Paris. Yolande, Madeleine, and Eliane had been captured, respectively, in January (St. Quentin), February (Chartres), and March (Marseilles) of 1944. Again, it was just as well that I did not know this at the time.

After Falaise things seemed more straightforward, and as the American soldier at Vire had suggested might happen, there were Allied trucks heading into Paris. I was very grateful to get a lift with one of them. I knew of only one place in Paris I wanted to go to, and that was La Coupole. By now my feet, in Bertha's shoes, were horribly blistered, and I could hardly walk. As I stumbled on, I thought of Bertha, and of the person before her who had used these shoes.

Within twenty minutes of walking from where the truck dropped me I had reached Montparnasse, my old neighborhood. Walking in the door of La Coupole was surreal. I stood still, gazing at the 1930s décor that was so familiar to me. And Ivan was there—dependable, lovely Ivan. I must have looked horrendous, but I didn't see that reflected on his face. I was waiflike by then, having lost almost twenty-five pounds since being dropped in back in May, five months before. Ivan scooped me up in a big hug, and announced to anyone who was within earshot that I was there, adding: "She is the best soldier that I've ever known." It was much what he had said the last time I had seen him in Paris, though in the state I was in I felt anything but. Ivan looked so proud of me, and at the same time so relieved. Maybe that was how I felt, too, but I was too exhausted to express anything at that moment.

At the back of La Coupole there was a room with a bed in it, and Ivan took me there and told me to go to sleep. I felt safe. For the first time in five months, I *knew* I was safe. I was asleep within moments.

* * *

MUCH TO MY DELIGHT, when I woke up, Katia was there. Ivan had contacted her. She had reached Paris quite some time before, having caught rides with the Allies much earlier than I had. She had news, too: the British had taken over a hotel close by—Hôtel Cecil— and Buckmaster had arrived there a couple of days ago. I had no idea why he was here or how long he was to stay, but I knew it was imperative that I see him.

"Do you think de Baissac is there?" I ventured.

"I doubt it," Katia replied. "He and Lise had their uniforms sent over when they heard that Paris was about to be freed, and wanted to make sure they were here for the liberation in August. You know him—he was always mouthing off about de Gaulle, calling him a coward while men like him were fighting in France, and guess what?"

"What?" I asked.

"That got back to the man himself—de Gaulle made a point of kicking him out!"

We laughed. Loudly. It was the strangest emotion to experience. It felt like we were two silly schoolgirls giggling about something inane. When we calmed down, Katia added that there was lots of tension between SOE and de Gaulle, so we were probably not welcome in Paris. It might be best if we quietly found Buckmaster and got out of there.

At the door of the hotel there was a snotty-nosed English Army chap who would not let us in through the main doors even though we asked for Buckmaster by name. He kept saying that the hotel was off-limits to nonmilitary personnel like us. To come this far and not be able to report back to the man who had hired me was unthinkable.

Eventually I said: "I want you to take a specific message to a man called Buckmaster. And that is that Pippa is here."

He reluctantly agreed and sent a colleague indoors with the message. When this man came out again and whispered in the snotty one's ear, he just said, "Oh, you can go in now."

No apology, nothing.

"But not you," he added, pointing to Katia.

"No—she is coming with me," was my swift reply. He did not stop us.

The doors opened onto a lobby that was full of people smoking,

227

creating a real haze. Out of the smoke I saw the familiar shape of Buckmaster coming toward me. I was beyond everything now; I couldn't even take another step. Buckmaster came straight up and gave me an enveloping hug—and that's when I started crying. His sympathy tipped me over the edge.

I pulled myself together, saying, "This is stupid. I should be laughing."

Still holding my bony little shoulders, Buckmaster looked at me and said, "Tears for courage are never wasted, Pippa."

In his eyes I could see a real sense of relief that one of his own had come home safely. There was empathy for what I had endured, and reassurance that all would be alright now.

"We will get you back home, but first let's get you to a hospital," he said, passing me over to the ladies from the Red Cross who had suddenly appeared out of nowhere.

It had been two months since I had sent the message to home base to say I was leaving Champgenéteux for Paris. ETA IMI. That arrival date was now known—October 5, 1944.

FIFTEEN

HELLO, ENGLAND

I WAS IN THE HOSPITAL IN PARIS FOR THREE DAYS. THE first task was to bathe me, because I had been in the same clothes for the past three weeks. I think I must have stunk a bit. Unfortunately, the whole of Paris was short of water, so the Red Cross ladies had to bathe me in a little cut-off wine barrel only about a foot deep. I stood in it, and they used a jug to scoop water up and pour it over my head in an attempt to get my hair halfway clean. Then I had to try to sit in the thing to get the rest of me washed properly.

I was put into a bed after the bath, but couldn't sleep. Whether it was an aftereffect of the Benzedrine or the busyness of my brain, that was the start of my insomnia. For months afterward, I could not sleep. I would just doze, feeling like I was sleeping, but when I "woke up" it would only have been six or seven minutes of drifting off. I never got into a deep sleep. It is torturous, the lack of sleep.

Katia came to see me in the hospital, and I asked her if she would be coming to England.

"Well, maybe," she replied. "But before I even think about that I need to go back to Italy to try and find my husband." He had been fighting there, and I imagine she must have wondered if he was even alive—not that she ever burdened me with her worries. I wanted England to be an option for her and decided to put a good word in when I got back.

I also floated another option. "What if, when you find him, you came and lived in Africa?" I suggested.

She laughed at that rather crazy thought until I convinced her it was not a scary place. Mostly. For myself, I could not wait to get back to Africa. The wide-open plains held such great memories for me, and I wanted to be back in them. I knew that France was not a country I ever wanted to return to, and apart from the odd necessary refueling stop—where I never left the airport—I intentionally never have.

After seventy-two hours I was deemed in good enough shape to fly back to London, from Le Bourget airport, on October 9, 1944. They had to get me a uniform to wear, and the smallest size available was a man's uniform. When I put the pants on, they fell straight down to my ankles. Some suspenders were found to keep them up on my tiny little seventy-three-pound frame, but I did look a bit ridiculous. And that's how I arrived in England—in a man's army uniform that was way too big.

One of the first things I wanted to sort out was the location of the items I had left with Simone. They were important mementos of mine. I asked Buckmaster to check with Claude about the whereabouts of my gold pen and powder compact and have them returned to me. The answer I received was that he had not taken them and that (of course) it was *my* responsibility to retrieve them. There seemed to be no redress; he had won. The Bastard—that was what I called him. I suspected he had stolen the compact to give to his sister. He may have kept the pen for himself, or sold it for personal gain; I don't know.

Buckmaster also told me he had been back personally to see Paul the previous month after the Allies had gone through, and the area had settled down. Paul was safe and well, as was his family. So too was the Baguenard family. I was very relieved.

The next thing was to sort out a way to get Katia to England. I requested that she be allowed to come and stay in England if she so wished, and the initial impression I got was that this would not be a problem. However, Katia later sent me a telegram saying that England had refused to honor the promise to let her in. I thought that was thoroughly petty after all she had done for England.

✦ ✦ ✦

IT TOOK ME QUITE some time to regain my strength and put weight back on, but when finally I was deemed well enough, I was back in training. From January 1945, I underwent arduous review courses and again spent time in the secretive "Stately 'omes of England." My report from STS 35—Beaulieu—noted that I had a good memory, knew my own mind, and was able to look after myself. I had made it known that I did not want to be an organizer, but just to perform my radio operator duties and let someone else deal with all that stuff in the field.

They also wrote that I was determined to succeed.

Then I was back to STS 51 (Dunham House) for more parachute training. They observed that I had improved since my first training there and that, "although rather thin with very little flesh covering her bones, she landed very lightly, and the actual descents were highly satisfactory." It was a completely different experience from my first time parachute training and I thoroughly enjoyed it. So much so that I asked to do four rather than the regulatory three jumps that women were allowed. As that would have set a precedent for women, however, the request was denied. I did get a first-class pass this time, though, which pleased me immensely. After my refresher, which lasted for the first three months of 1945, I was briefed to go back into the field—a parachute jump into Germany, under a new code name. This was to be Routal, which is (almost) Latour spelled backward. My mission was to help get a Polish family out before the Russians arrived, because the family had been working for SOE. By the time the mission was ready to go, though, the rapid advance of the Allies made it unnecessary and it was called off.

When I was told, I was relieved. I was so grateful to be done with war. I heard that the Polish man got out, but his wife and children were caught. They ended up in Siberia, I think.

On April 30, 1945, Hitler committed suicide in his bunker in Berlin as the Soviet forces closed in on the city. A week later, on May 7, Germany officially surrendered to the Allies. Churchill spoke to the nation, inspiring the masses below and all around the globe:

God bless you all. This is your victory! It is the victory of the cause of freedom in every land. In all our long history we have never seen a greater day than this. Everyone, man or woman, has done their best. Everyone has tried.

"Land of Hope and Glory" was sung at full volume by the crowd below. It was a moment to behold. VE (Victory in Europe) Day on May 8 was an ecstatic event. It marked the formal acceptance, by the Allies of World War II, of Germany's unconditional surrender of its armed forces and the official end of World War II in Europe.

London was awash with the Union Jack, and the skyline was lit up with searchlights and fireworks. Londoners took to the streets in huge numbers—singing, dancing, laughing, living. There were street parties, people dancing the conga around bonfires, and the V for Victory sign was everywhere. The images of the crowds in Piccadilly Circus, Trafalgar Square, and other landmarks were incredible.

It would be another three months until VJ (Victory in Japan) day, on August 15, 1945, after the US dropped bombs on Hiroshima (August 6) and Nagasaki (August 9). The formal surrender ceremony that took place on USS *Missouri* in Tokyo Bay on September 2 officially ended World War II.

☆ ☆ ☆

ALSO IN 1945, THE last of the captive F Section SOE women died. On her second mission, Violette Szabo had been captured at Salon-la-Tour in June 1944. Denise Bloch was also captured that month, at Sermaise, and Lilian Rolfe a month later in July 1944 at Nangis. All three were executed at Ravensbrück concentration camp around February 5, 1945, shot in the back of the head. Hitler's "Commando Order" of 1942 was still being carried out even as late as then—six months after Paris had been freed, for goodness' sake! No rules of war, no Geneva Convention. The fact that they just kept on carrying out Hitler's order even though the end was clearly nigh is appalling to me. We all knew that being tortured and executed was possible, but I had suppressed, somewhere deep down, the thought of it ever happening to me. I simply concentrated on surviving every day and not getting caught.

Yvonne Rudellat died in captivity of typhus, on April 24, 1945, in Bergen-Belsen, eight days after the liberation of the camp. She had been captured almost two years previously, in June 1943, at Bracieux. And lastly there was Cecily Lefort, who was captured at Montéli-mar in September 1943. She died in the gas chamber at the Ucker-mark Youth Camp, adjacent to Ravensbrück, on May 1, 1945. The day after Hitler killed himself.

The treatment these women endured before they died was horrific. I could say so much more, but it would be disturbing. Please read about it, read about them all. Lovely Lilian. To think her dad thought she was being posted to a safer job in England. Our time together as we started our SOE journey seemed a lifetime ago. I had survived, unlike these poor women for whom I have the utmost respect.

★ ★ ★

I HAD NOT COME through unscathed, though, and that became evident very quickly. Flashbacks started soon after I got back to England, and they have stayed with me my entire life. I am thankful I had never needed to be violent there and I never killed anyone—I would not want to relive moments like those again and again.

Anything will set me off. A smell, a baby crying, somebody in front of me walking a certain way—and I am back in France in a second even though I am awake. Sometimes they come in my sleep and I wake up in a lather of sweat. Completely drenched.

It is always the same. I hear somebody breathing and I've got to catch up with that person to stop them going somewhere. I follow the breathing, and then we come to several roads and I'm not sure which one the breathing took, and so I'm in a real panic. If only I could find out who the breather is—but there's no person there and I must stop them. And of course, when I wake up, I won't go back to sleep at all because it might just carry on. So I spend the whole night awake, thinking about it.

I talked to the air-force psychiatrist about it, and we thought it might have come from when I aborted the Jedburgh landing with the S-Phone. In June 1945 my file notes that "since the collapse of Germany Miss Latour has suffered from severe nervous strain. She has recently passed through the hands of the Air Ministry psychiatrist, who has recommended that she be released from the WAAF immediately." In September that year I would also be made an Honorary Section Officer in the WAAF—not that it would mean much to me by then, because I would be back in my beloved Africa. I was released from service in July 1945.

I was pleased to have my service come to an end. I was questioned about my time in the field for my record, and told them everything they needed to know. An exit interview, as they'd call it these days. They noted down that I had sent 135 messages and was to be awarded an MBE for my efforts for the empire. I had also asked that Katia be recognized as someone who had helped me, as my courier, and also took the opportunity to make it known that Mme. Durand, the daughter of my "grandparents," should also be recognized for her good work. Early in the war, in 1940 she hid escaped French prisoners and helped them get to unoccupied France with false papers. When I was there in 1944, she stood guard while I sent messages and helped with the hiding of sets and batteries while visiting her parents' home. Her husband was a suspected collaborator so she separated from him in 1942, dedicating herself to the liberation cause.

When I finally got hold of my file, in my nineties, I smiled wryly when I read one comment: "I think Scientist [Claude de Baissac] must have been very unpleasant to work with." They assumed correctly.

* * *

AS I GOT MYSELF ready to leave England in late 1945, I found two precious items I had put aside for safekeeping: the beautiful red shoes I had bought in London just before I left, and the lucky monkey-foot charm given to me by Nyama Njoka in the Belgian Congo. As a pair, they looked utterly incongruous.

I could not imagine ever again wearing anything as beautiful as those shoes. Perhaps a time might come again when all I had to focus on was putting on a pretty dress and those gorgeous red wedges, but it seemed to be for a different Pippa. I would take them with me, though—the future Pippa might want them.

I rolled the lucky charm around in my hand, smelled it, and then closed my eyes and said a silent thank-you. Nyama had said it would keep me safe, and it had. That would definitely be making the trip back to Africa.

When I first returned to the Belgian Congo, I stayed with a childhood friend, a Greek chap who owned a store there. I could see that the unrest was still there and it would probably be wise to move to the Serengeti plains to be with Aunt Ada and Uncle Eric. Their home was like my home, and the freedom and majesty of the animals that surrounded it was something I loved. It grounded me. In my mind I could take myself back there at any time, and in wartime I often had. I had often imagined what that life would be like again. Could I ever have that life back? It turned out that I could!

Dealing with war had been exhausting. I was so sick of double agents, collaborators, the fact that you couldn't trust anybody, all that sort of thing. And so once I was back in Africa, I consciously made some personal rules for myself. The war's finished. Think that it never happened. Put it out of your mind. And that's why I never talked about it. Never. It was to be buried away and forgotten, and only spoken about with those who had been there or truly understood it.

I also contacted Katia again to check whether she and her husband (she had indeed found him) would like to come and live in Africa with me after all. I was honest about the unrest bubbling away and the potential of conflict. Katia's reply was simple. It was a nice offer but she and her husband would like to stay in Italy. "We've had enough. Enough war. There is no more in me." She finished her letter by asking me if I would like instead to move to Italy. I did not, as my own home was Africa. I just needed to find family again, and a more peaceful part of it to live in.

Before I moved, yet again, there was one last visit I needed to make and that was to Nyama Njoka, the healer who had given me the lucky monkey's foot when I first left the Belgian Congo at the age of twelve. I was now twenty-four.

I found him in the place I had expected to find him. He was older and more wizened, but other than that he looked just the same to me. Nyama recognized me immediately. His wide, toothless grin of welcome told me so, along with his laugh and a gesture with his hand that went from his hip to his head. Yes, I had certainly grown taller in that time. I was older, maybe wiser, and most definitely disenchanted with man's inhumanity to man. We spoke briefly, in Swahili, before I pulled out the precious token he had given me all those years ago. Given to a concerned twelve-year-old leaving the only country this man had ever known. Nyama nodded his head sagely and took it. I told him of the many places it had protected me from harm, and how grateful I was that he had placed that spell on it all those years ago. In my logical mind I knew that I had been the master of my own destiny and that life events were not purely fateful or predestined, but there was also a part of me that wondered about all that. Perhaps there *was* something in it.

He carefully examined the monkey's foot. I thought he might reimbue it with something magical, and was half expecting a similar event to the one when he'd gifted it to me twelve years ago. But instead, he threw it violently to the ground, grabbed a heavy instrument, and proceeded to destroy it, then kicked the remains away.

He then solemnly announced: "You have no need of this now. It has done its job."

And with that assurance from Nyama, I left the Belgian Congo for Kenya. My life was in my hands now, and it was up to me to make of it what I wanted. I was ready to write the next chapter of whatever my unusual life would bring me.

EPILOGUE

THE TROUBLES IN THE BELGIAN CONGO CONTINUED after Pippa arrived back in Africa after the war, and she moved to Dar es Salaam—a coastal town in Tanzania. Unbeknownst to her when she was young, a house in what was then Tanganyika had been left to her at the age of eight by a relative and had been kept in trust for her.

Aunt Ada and Uncle Eric were still on the Serengeti, a constant in her life. They were still taking tourists on safari and doing game-warden work. Pippa loved reconnecting with wildlife, and was moved when a lion she had looked after as a cub back in her teen years came back to the house one day to lie down beside her. The regal lioness remembered Pippa and greeted her like a long-lost friend. Pippa had another pet cheetah, often used as a hunting companion, although sadly a tourist on safari shot and killed it by mistake. She was heartbroken—she loved her cheetah and treated it like a pet dog.

Pippa took up formal flying training, going solo in November 1946 using her Uncle Eric's plane. She became the first female licensed pilot in East Africa. She bought a wooden "juju" box for good luck, which she kept for years but finally burned one day when she was going through a rough patch, saying that it had obviously run out of luck.

Pippa chose never to set foot back in France. She married Paddy Doyle, an engineer, in Kenya in 1948. Their first two children, Barry and Pauline, were born there. After they moved to Australia for his work, they had two more children—Odette and Brendon. Paulette's name lived on through Pauline and Odette. Just like her mother before her, all of Pippa's babies were born a couple of months early.

The family later had another move, to Fiji, again following a work opportunity for Paddy. The marriage was shaky, however, and one day in 1959, aged thirty-eight, Pippa decided to take matters into her own hands and move back to Australia with the children. In her haste, though, she ended up on the wrong flight—which she found out, midflight, was destined for Auckland, New Zealand, rather than Brisbane, Australia. With just ninety-eight dollars in her purse, she decided to stay anyway and make New Zealand her home.

Pippa never told her husband and children about her SOE work, saying only that she was a balloon operator in the war. In the early 2000s, however, her sons found something about her on the internet, and when asked if it was true she confessed that it was. She continued to choose not to speak publicly about her SOE experience except on rare occasions. "People would ask me, 'How many Germans did you kill?' And I would say, 'Well I didn't kill any, but my radio killed a few thousand,' and usually leave it at that." Others spoke, books were written, things were said, but Pippa stayed quiet. However, early on she was unhappy that Lise had been identified as her courier in some publications, so she appealed to Maurice Buckmaster to correct the record to Katia, asking him to verify the fact with Claude de Baissac as head of the Scientist network.

The baby that was in Simone Baguenard's arms when Pippa had first met her in Champgenéteux grew up to become father to a man called Fabien. He wrote to Pippa on behalf of his grandmother, who was wondering what had happened to Paulette, the secret agent who sent messages from her attic. In part, this was prompted by the death of her husband, Georges, in 1995, when an old farmer who attended his funeral asked if anybody knew whether Paulette had survived the walk to Paris, and if she had, where she might be in the world. Pippa suspected that that man might have been one of the two old farmers on one of Paul Janvier's mother's farms who were in the same Resistance network as Simone and Georges. It took Fabien three years of research to find "Paulette" and get a letter to her on behalf of his grandmother. When the letter finally reached Pippa, she was delighted to reconnect with Simone. Pippa recalled talking to her on the phone and Simone asking her, "Are you as ugly as I am, now we are both so old?"—to which she laughed and said, "Yes!" Neither of them had dared to presume that they would survive World War II, let alone have the opportunity to grow old. Their reconnection made Simone extremely happy, just a few days before she died in 2007.

☆ ☆ ☆

VERA ATKINS STAYED IN touch with Pippa, as she did with all of the surviving women of F Section. She and Pippa became personal friends, with Vera coming out to see her in Africa and Australia each time she had a baby. "It was an excuse to see a new country." Commissioned as a squadron leader in the WAAF—she had spent the war as a civilian—Vera went to Germany in 1946 with a list of 118 missing F agents (including 14 women). When she came back, a year later, she had crossed 117 names off the list. She was determined to find out how they died, visiting concentration camps and interrogating guards and Nazi war-crimes suspects—including Rudolf Höss, ex-commandant of Auschwitz-Birkenau.

Pippa stayed in contact with Yvonne Baseden and Sonia Butt, as the SOE agents who were the younger ones like herself. Many became obscure and melted back into society, never wanting to talk about their experience openly, as was Pippa's modus operandi. Pippa and Yvonne would sometimes muse in their old age on whether either of them would hold the record of being the oldest-surviving F Section woman. They ended up being the last two left. Pippa said, "Nancy Wake and Lise de Baissac held the record at ninety-eight, so we were aiming for ninety-nine. It was me who eventually won that honor, turning ninety-nine in 2020. Yvonne died at age ninety-five in 2017, and was pleased to have had the chance to grow old. She had cheated death at Ravensbrück, the largest women-only concentration camp within Germany's prewar borders. To survive that hellish place, with its torture for SOE agents as part and parcel of the vile experience, was unusual."

When medals were being proposed postwar, Pippa recalled a discussion about the prospect of awarding the George Cross to all radio operators. That did not eventuate, and only three were awarded to F Section SOE agents—Odette Sansom in 1946 and, posthumously, Violette Szabo in 1946 and Noor Inayat-Khan in 1949. At the time, Pippa was adamant that: "Even if it was offered to us all, I would refuse it because Katia wouldn't get it. We were a pair, and I was never going to accept anything until Katia had the same as me." When it was agreed that Katia would be recognized with a (civil) MBE for her service, Pippa agreed to receive her (military) MBE, which was awarded by King George VI in September 1945. "Whatever she got I would take," Pippa said. However, she did not want to attend a ceremony to have it bestowed, instead asking for it to be posted to her via the Special Forces Club, who sent it on to her in Africa. Her campaign medals were also sent that way, as well as the Croix de Guerre avec Palme en Bronze for bravery in January 1946.

In November 2014, inside "Rennie Lines" (home to the Special Air Service at Papakura Military Camp, in Auckland), French Ambassador Laurent Contini bestowed France's highest military decoration on Pippa. The Chevalier de l'Ordre national de la Légion d'honneur (Knight of the National Order of the Legion of Honour) was awarded for her service in occupied France. The ceremony was attended by her two sons. In 2017 Pippa received the French Brevet militaire de parachutiste (French parachute wings), saying that at ninety-six she was honored to be receiving her wings.

Pippa would wear her medals at appropriate occasions (on the left, as per protocol if you yourself have been awarded them). She recalled an occasion when an older man came up to her and said, "My dear, I'm telling you they should be on the right. You should not be wearing your husband's medals on the left." Pippa replied with: "Well, can you unpin it for me?" He duly did so and repinned them on her right-hand side. Pippa's rationale was that: "He was such a dear old man I wasn't going to say anything." Somebody later that day informed him of Pippa's history, and he came to her in tears, mortified that he had presumed they were not hers. He wanted to put them back on the correct side for her, but Pippa suggested she might just take them off, which she did for the rest of the event.

Pippa had a Cross of Lorraine made, which she always wore as a reminder of the French Resistance. The Free French forces had adopted the symbol on July 1, 1940, as a response to the Nazi swastika. It was later generally adopted throughout Free France as a symbol of resistance. A fifty-nine-foot cross can be found on one of the Normandy landing beaches on the spot where General de Gaulle landed on June 14, 1944. An even larger Cross of Lorraine, over 140 feet high, was erected in de Gaulle's home village of Colombey-les-Deux-Églises in the Champagne-Ardenne region of France. Asked why she wore hers, Pippa said, "Well, it means quite a bit to me because I know the history of it. Other people don't. It never leaves me. The only time I've taken it off is if I had to be x-rayed or scanned." Both of these events rarely happened to Pippa.

SOE was dissolved on January 15, 1946. MI6 absorbed some of its people; others went back to the remarkably diverse callings from which they had come. Very few SOE records have survived. A fire in November 1945 at the War Office Record Center destroyed a lot of military records, and with the dissolution of SOE shortly thereafter, the archiving of their files, and decisions around what to keep, was ad hoc at best.

Colin Gubbins, Director General of SOE, overrode the fears of the security staff and encouraged the setting-up of the Special Forces Club in London in a nondescript, unnamed building close to Harrods in London. It has provided a place where old members of SOE—and other aligned bodies such as SAS, SBS, and MI9—can gather. The walls are adorned with multiple portraits of SOE members, and the company at the bar is always interesting. The Special Forces Club became the gatekeeper for any communication with

Pippa, and they stayed in touch, with the liaison officer visiting her in New Zealand regularly.

When the former Royal New Zealand Air Force base at Hobsonville in Auckland, New Zealand, was decommissioned and made into a residential area, Genevieve Lane was named in Pippa's honor in a ceremony she attended in March 2020. Pippa was a member of her local Returned and Services Association military support charity, who offered her free meals should she want them. The New Zealand Special Air Services adopted her as one of their own, and twice a year would send a team of people around to her remote property to cut down trees and do work around the grounds. Pippa lived independently at her rural home among the flocks of birds she fed twice a day with the specially made bird-feeder on her deck, with Coco her elderly dog her constant companion. She did not have the internet or a mobile phone. Pippa first got COVID-19 just six months before she died and was hospitalized for two days as a precaution, but got out as soon as she could—"Because you could get sick there." The staff called her a wonder woman.

Pippa had left the Catholic Church, unhappy with the Pope sympathizing with Nazis after the war, and "chose to be a free thinker." Her instructions for her funeral were that it could be anything but a Catholic service. "I'm not an atheist or anything—I can do any of them apart from Catholicism, because of what happened with them after World War II, hiding Nazis."

Pippa passed away peacefully on October 7, 2023, and she was farewelled at a small, private funeral. She was not only the last SOE F Section agent of the (39) women to die, but the last SOE of all of F Section (430 people) to pass away.

Pippa Latour—the last secret agent.

ACKNOWLEDGMENTS

SADLY, PIPPA PASSED AWAY BEFORE THIS BOOK WENT to print; so in a departure from the norm, I, as her writer, would like to recognize a few people on Pippa's behalf whom I know she would want to acknowledge. I am quite sure there are people she would have thanked in a wider sense, but these reflections are specifically in relation to this memoir.

Pippa made it abundantly clear to me that she would only talk about her life if the fourteen brave SOE women who died were acknowledged. She had huge respect for them and wanted people to know about their sacrifice far more than she wanted to talk about her own experiences.

She also wanted people to understand how wonderful the FANYs (First Aid Nursing Yeomanry) were. Her relief at knowing that someone was always there waiting for her to connect gave her great comfort. After the war they stayed in touch, and just before Pippa died I was very pleased to meet Sumitra Tikaram (Sumi) on her behalf at the Special Forces Club in London. Sumi was the SOE FANY liaison in London, who in Pippa had one last secret agent to look after. Pippa was not only the last of the SOE F (French) Section women to die, but also the last of all 430 F Section agents, thus putting a close to an era of history.

Putting Pippa's memoir together has been quite the task, and we needed the help of Peter Wheeler, former longtime CEO of New Zealand Bomber Command Association, Inc. Peter spent quite some time with Pippa over the years, talking to her and making notes about her life that Pippa then corroborated. He also requested Pippa's SOE files for her to see. She enjoyed having the folders he put together for her to look through. I have hugely valued Peter's wisdom and his knowledge of World War II and of Pippa's life when going through the material.

David Harrison, a UK historian with a particular interest in the F Section of SOE, has also been of great support. He met Pippa on a trip to New Zealand and has been very helpful sourcing various SOE records and answering my many questions as I connected official records with Pippa's memories. He assured me that he welcomed questions, so I kept asking them! I am also grateful for his connections to specialists in World War II radio sets, access to people who wrote about other people in this time period, and his most wonderful library of books.

Pippa wanted to acknowledge David Hopkins, her friend and military colleague. David always had Pippa's best interests at heart, looking after all her affairs and helping get her the support and recognition she deserved in military circles and beyond. Service, ethics, and duty are traits they shared in spades. Lyn Macdonald, Pippa's longtime friend, reassured Pippa that her life story would be interesting and inspiring for people to read; and Brendon, Pippa's younger son, was a constant on my many visits to Pippa and a great protector of her when she was unwell. Pippa told me how grateful she was to them both for their love and support.

It must be noted that this is not a biography with every detail cross-referenced, but rather Pippa's personal memoir, based on a series of conversations with her. I am not a historian. I am simply a writer who enjoys helping other people find their voice. Pippa primarily wanted to do this to "get her feelings out" about the first twenty-five years of her life. While some things were still in sharp focus at the ages of 101 and then 102, there were obviously gaps in Pippa's memory and knowledge. Pippa's memoir has therefore been constructed from a profusion of sources, and dialogue has been reconstructed in places in the interest of the story.

It has been quite an undertaking, and so I imagine Pippa would also thank me for the time and effort that has gone into producing her memoir as a record of her unusual childhood and war service. I think she would probably add that she secretly loved the cheese scones and other yummy morsels I would bring to our numerous chats. She would tell me I didn't need to bring anything, but they always got eaten so I kept bringing them. Pippa also got used to our selfies, often directing me to move back so I didn't look like a giant.

I know Pippa would join me in thanking editor Teresa McIntyre for her experienced eye in reviewing the final manuscript, and Michelle Hurley, Leanne McGregor, and the rest of the team at Allen & Unwin New Zealand for pulling the book together. A special thank-you to Dean Buchanan who initially reached out to Michelle to see if there was interest in Pippa's story, and to Michelle for giving me the (unexpected) opportunity to help Pippa bring her story to life.

* * *

ACKNOWLEDGMENTS

AND NOW I HAVE my own thanks to give, and those are to
Pippa. Firstly, for her patience with me! While she recalled numerous events and the people in them in detail over a huge period,
her expectation was that I would go away, do my research, and have
various conversations with people to find out more, corroborating
things as needed. She was very pleased with me on successive visits
when I had "got it," or discovered something she wanted to know, or
provided information that was new to her. I valued her book collection, along with her guidance on which books and anecdotes within
them were "poppycock" and which were reliable to read. I noted her
handwritten notes on some, correcting what was published. They
have been dipped into on multiple occasions. At the time of our
putting together this memoir, Pippa was keenly aware that she was
102, and she warned me: "I could drop down dead in the middle of
this sentence, so we'd better get on with it!" Some tasks that she set
me were, however, impossible, like getting "poppycock" about her
removed from the internet. "Poppycock" was a favorite word she
would use about things she knew not to be right.

Secondly, I want to thank her for her friendship on this journey
together and her excitement at my travels to France and England
to discover her past. When I showed her videos of (what had been)
RAF Tempsford, she was back there in an instant. A special thank-
you to Steve Cooney for making that happen. Simone and Georges
Baguenard had provided safe haven for Pippa in Champgenéteux
in 1944, and she was delighted when I tracked down their grandson
Fabien in Canada. She was thrilled to hear from him by email (via
me, as she had no email or internet) and see photos of the village
from back in her time. I visited this village in France and showed
her video of where she had been seventy-nine years before, which

fascinated her. Neighboring Bais (home of Dr. Paul Janvier, the leader of the local Resistance network) had a little library that was open, and I am hugely grateful to the librarian who gave me a copy of his memoir, which covered Pippa's time there. It has been incredibly helpful in corroborating Pippa's story. I delivered Pippa a copy (in French), which she was very pleased to have. It was also wonderful to be able to pass on to Pippa that she was the topic of conversation around the table at the Special Forces Club in London when I caught up with Sumi, her FANY SOE liaison officer.

Finally, I want to thank Pippa for her bravery in telling her story. It has been such a privilege to hear, and I hope I have done it justice. As I said to her, it is important that future generations know what went on—and she agreed that it was good to make them aware, but she hoped she would be dead when it came out! Privacy was important to Pippa (and in that regard I am quite sure there are some things she has not mentioned here), so a published memoir would have been bothersome to her inherently private nature.

Pippa and I refining our selfie technique throughout 2023.
(Jude Dobson)

There are many lessons to learn from Pippa's remarkable life: about reliable adults forming attachments with children that make them feel loved and confident for a lifetime; the value of resilience in challenging times; the fostering of self-reliance; maintaining hope for a better tomorrow, and playing an active part in creating that future; doing something for the greater good; and being brave.

Pippa got her wish—she is not here to see her memoir go to print. She left a lasting impression on me, as I am quite sure she will on others through this memoir. I will miss our chats. Thank you for your service, Pippa. Godspeed.

Jude Dobson
March 2024

APPENDIX I

PIPPA'S SERVICE DETAILS AND HONORS

Our thanks to Pippa's friend and military colleague David Hopkins for compiling this list.

MILITARY RANKS

Leading Aircraftwoman (LACW) in Women's Auxiliary Air Force (WAAF): September 23, 1943

Honorary Commission: Acting Section Officer in Special Operations Executive (SOE): March 31, 1944

Section Officer in SOE: June 16, 1944

WORLD WAR II OPERATIONAL SERVICE

Military Service WWII: 1941–1945

Special Operations Executive (SOE) Operative: September 23, 1943–July 7, 1945

SERVICE/BRANCH AND REGIMENTAL NUMBERS

Women's Auxiliary Air Force (WAAF), Royal Air Force (RAF),
Service No. 718483

First Aid Nursing Yeomanry (FANY), Service No. 8108

Special Operations Executive (SOE) Field Operator, Regt. No.
9909

BRITISH HONORS, AWARDS, AND MEDALLIC RECOGNITION

Member of the Order of the British Empire (MBE Military),
medal est. June 4, 1917, by King George V, awarded September 4,
1954

Military Campaign Medal: 1939–1945 Star

Military Campaign Medal: France and Germany Star

Military Campaign Medal: Defense Medal (United Kingdom)
Military Campaign Medal: War Medal 1939–1945

Brevet British Parachute Wings (Operational Jump Wings)

FRENCH HONORS, AWARDS, AND MEDALLIC RECOGNITION

Croix de Guerre avec Palme en Bronze (War Cross with Bronze
Palm 1935–1939), awarded by French government January 16,
1946

Chevalier de l'Ordre national de la Légion d'honneur (Knight of
the National Order of the Legion of Honour), medal est. 1802
by Napoleon Bonaparte, awarded by French ambassador to
New Zealand November 25, 2014

Brevet militaire de parachutiste (French parachute wings),
awarded by French ambassador to New Zealand October 5,
2017

OTHER

In November 2004, Pippa opened a New Zealand Special Operations Executive (SOE) memorial at Papakura Military Camp,
alongside WWII SOE Commander Lt. Col. Arthur Edmonds,
who served in occupied Greece. The memorial area includes
a brick on the "NZSAS Pathways of Memories" with Pippa's
name and regt. number.

On March 1, 2020, Genevieve Lane in Hobsonville was opened on
the site of the decommissioned Royal New Zealand Air Force
(RNZAF) base. The new street was named in recognition of
Pippa's war service (Geneviève being her SOE field name) and
Pippa attended the ceremony.

Since 2002, in honor of Pippa, the New Zealand Special Air Service (NZSAS) has awarded the "Section Officer Pippa Doyle
Award for Innovation" annually to a serving officer or soldier
of 1st New Special Air Service Regiment (1 NZSAS Regt.).

APPENDIX II

SOE MEMORIALS

- The Valençay SOE Memorial in France honors 104 SOE agents (91 men and 13 women) of F Section who lost their lives while working in France. It was opened in 1991. (Note that Sonia Olschanezky would bring the number of women to 14; she is missing from the memorial because she was not officially trained as an SOE agent. However, after her arrest she was treated as if she was an SOE agent and was executed alongside three female SOE agents, so we include her in our numbers elsewhere.)
- The official memorial to all those who served in SOE during World War II was unveiled on February 13, 1996, on the wall of the west cloister of Westminster Abbey in London, by Queen Elizabeth, the Queen Mother.
- A further memorial to SOE's agents was unveiled in October 2009 on the Albert Embankment in London.
- The Tempsford Memorial with the quote "By the full moon

we flew" was unveiled on December 3, 2013, by Charles, the then–Prince of Wales, in Church End, Tempsford, Bedfordshire. It is close to the site of the former RAF Tempsford airfield and Gibraltar Farm, where Pippa took off from in England, and her name is on the memorial.

- A memorial on the outer wall of St. Paul's church in Knightsbridge, London, honors the FANY women who died in World War II, including those who were female agents of SOE F Section. It was unveiled on May 7, 1948.

ON FACING PAGE

The Tempsford Memorial in Bedfordshire. Pippa's name appears fourth from the top. (*Steve Cooney*)

OVERLEAF

Gibraltar Farm, on the site of RAF Tempsford, photographed in modern times. The plaque on the wall inside states: "Erected to commemorate the brave deeds of the men and women of every nationality who flew from this wartime airfield to the forces of the Resistance in France, Norway, Holland, and other countries during the years 1942 to 1945. The equipment for their dangerous missions was issued to them from this barn."

TOP: (*Jude Dobson*) BOTTOM: (*David Harrison*)

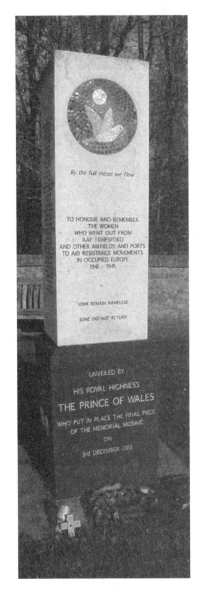

APPENDIX III

WOMEN AGENTS OF SOE F SECTION

The following is an extract from a table compiled by UK historian David Harrison, a meticulous researcher with a special interest in the F Section of SOE. Our thanks go to David for allowing us to reproduce this information in the book.

Surname	Forenames	Field Name	Operational Name	Main Network	Role	Nationality	Fate
Agazarian	Françoise (Françine) Isabella	Marguerite	Lamplighter	Prosper-Physician	Courier	British	Returned
Aisner	Julienne Marie Louise (JuJu)	Claire	Compositor	Farrier	Courier	French	Returned
Baseden	Yvonne Jeanne Thérèse de Vibraye	Odette	Bursar	Scholar	Radio operator	British	Survived capture
Beekman	Yolande Elsa Maria	Mariette	Palmist	Musician	Radio operator	French	Executed
Bloch	Denise Madeleine	Ambroise	Secretary	Clergyman	Radio operator	French	Executed
Borrel	Andrée Raymonde	Denise	Whitebeam	Prosper-Physician	Courier	French	Executed
Butt	Sonia Esmée Florence	Blanche	Biographer	Headmaster	Courier	British	Released
Byck	Muriel Tamara	Violette	Benefactress	Ventriloquist	Radio operator	British	Died of illness (1944)
Charlet	Valentine Blanche	Christianne	Berberis	Ventriloquist	Courier	British	Escaped

Cormeau	Beatrice Yvonne	Annette	Fairy	Wheelwright	Radio operator	British	Returned
Damerment	Madeleine Léonie Zöe	Solange	Dancer	Bricklayer	Courier	French	Executed
De Baissac	Lise Marie Jeanette	Odile	Artist	Scientist 2	Organizer	Mauritian	Returned
Devereaux-Reynolds	Elizabeth	Elizabeth	Typist	Marksman	Courier	British/American	Survived capture
Fontaine	Yvonne	Mimi	Florist	Minister	Courier	French	Returned
Granville	Christine (Krystina)	Pauline	—	Jockey	Courier	Polish	Returned
Hall	Virginia	Marie	Heckler Geologist 5	Heckler Saint	Organizer	American	Returned
Herbert	Mary Katherine (Maureen)	Claudine	Jeweller	Scientist 1	Courier	British	Released
Inayat-Khan	Noor-un-nisa (Nora)	Madeleine	Nurse	Cinema-Phono	Radio operator	British	Executed
Jullian	Ginette Marie Hélène	Adèle	Janitress	Permit	Radio operator	British	Returned
Knight	Marguerite Diane Frances	Nicole	Kennelmaid	Donkeyman 2	Courier	British	Returned

Surname	Forenames	Field Name	Operational Name	Main Network	Role	Nationality	Fate
Latour	Phyllis Ada (Pippa)	Geneviève	Lampooner	Scientist 2	Radio operator	British	Returned
Lavigne	Madeleine	Isabelle	Leveller	Silversmith	Courier	French	Died of natural causes (1945)
Le Chene	Marie-Thérèse	Adèle	Wisteria	Plane	Courier	British	Returned
Lefort	Cicely Margot	Alice	Teacher	Jockey	Courier	British	Died in captivity
Leigh	Vera Eugenie	Simone	Almoner	Inventor	Courier	British	Executed
Nearne	Eileen Mary (Didi)	Rose	Pioneer	Wizard	Radio operator	British	Escaped
Nearne	Jacqueline Françoise Mary Josephine	Jacqueline	Designer	Stationer	Courier	British	Returned
O'Sullivan	Patricia (Paddy) Maureen	Josette	Stenographer	Fireman	Radio operator	British	Returned
Olschanezky	Sonia Sophie	Tania	—	Juggler	Courier	French	Executed

Plewman	Eliane Sophie	Gaby	Dean	Monk	Courier	British	Executed
Rolfe	Lilian Vera	Nadine	Recluse	Historian	Radio operator	British	Executed
Rowden	Diana Hope	Paulette	Chaplain	Acrobat	Courier	British	Executed
Rudellat	Yvonne Claire	Jacqueline	Soaptree	Prosper-Physician	Courier	British	Died in captivity
Sansom	Odette Marie Celine	Lise	Clothier	Spindle	Courier	British	Survived capture
Szabo	Violette Reine Elizabeth	Louise	Seamstress	Salesman 1 & 2	Courier	British	Executed
Wake	Nancy Grace Augusta	Hélène	Witch	Freelance	Courier	British	Returned
Walters	Anne-Marie	Colette	Milkmaid	Wheelwright	Courier	British	Returned
Wilen	Odette Victoria	Sophie	Waitress	Laborer	Radio operator	Finnish	Returned
Witherington	Cécile Pearl	Marie	Wrestler	Wrestler	Organizer	British	Returned

INDEX

ABOUT THE AUTHORS

Pippa Latour was the last surviving SOE agent, serving in France until its liberation. For seventy years, Pippa's contributions to the war effort were largely unheralded, but she was finally given her due in 2014 when she was awarded France's highest military decoration, the Chevalier de l'Ordre national de la Légion d'honneur (Knight of the National Order of the Legion of Honour). She died in 2023 at age 102.

Jude Dobson has been researching, writing, producing, and directing World War I and World War II content since 2018. Her audio documentary with New Zealand aviators reflecting on their wartime experiences won a New York Radio Award in 2023 for Best Historical Documentary.